UNTOLD.

The Campus Diaries

Karen Shayne and Lorna Dancey

ISBN 978-1-63885-837-9 (Paperback)
ISBN 978-1-63885-839-3 (Hardcover)
ISBN 978-1-63885-838-6 (Digital)

Copyright © 2021 Karen Shayne and Lorna Dancey
All rights reserved
First Edition

All rights reserved. No part of this publication may be reproduced, distributed, or transmitted in any form or by any means, including photocopying, recording, or other electronic or mechanical methods without the prior written permission of the publisher. For permission requests, solicit the publisher via the address below.

Covenant Books
11661 Hwy 707
Murrells Inlet, SC 29576
www.covenantbooks.com

To the thousands of college and university students who live each day with bravery, passion, and always with an UNTOLD story worth telling.

FOREWORD

> If we all could walk around with our stories written on our chests for everyone to read, we would all be much more compassionate, kinder, and less judgmental toward each other.

No one would have ever told us, several years ago, an introduction by a mutual friend would ignite a collaboration that would lead us to this beautiful path we now travel. Our vision was to create a global effort of building a bridge between our two countries through story sharing. While we may have been from different countries, we realized we were not so different from each other. As the words of our Untold stories share, that's how the beauty of the Untold project came to be.

Our hearts beat passionately to find and share hope through stories. Through *Untold*'s global storytelling movement, we mine the unknown tales of humanity and expose the remarkable stories of everyday people. We strive to give voice to life's diverse experiences, challenges, and vulnerabilities in a mission that ultimately can unite not just two countries but, today, the world.

Untold started as a safe place, free of judgment, to showcase heartfelt and hidden stories. As the blog grew, so did the project. As recent world events left our hearts broken, we felt growing compassion for the human spirit. From the icy-cold regions of Canada to the hot, muggy, Tennessee south, the *Untold* stories showcase grace and understanding to anyone who has ever had a challenge, celebration, crisis, or difficult patch on life's journey. *Untold* discovers the heart and hope of the human spirit, and through multiple platforms, we can now be part of the mission to address the societal issues that challenge today's monumental and controversial topics around mental health.

Granted, we didn't see the reach of *Untold* coming. But as we release our first book, we know there is so much left to share. We welcome everyone to join our movement to create awareness, seek change, and believe that the *Untold* story buried within everyone is a story that should be told.

Thank you for being part of the *Untold* project. We are grateful you are here. Thank you for your support to help two women find their way through each day to help build that bridge of hope—now across the world.

Karen and Lorna, UNTOLDProject.org

UNTOLD: THE CAMPUS DIARIES

While working on a spring 2020 internship for UNTOLD, a Middle Tennessee State University student proposed *UNTOLD: The Campus Diaries* as a mental health awareness campaign within the campus community. In a "Dear Diary" format, this online blog was designed to resonate with any student who has faced a challenge, crisis, or difficult period through their college years.

The result? Even with COVID-19 and nationwide campus shutdowns, students began submitting the powerful and moving stories of their mental health challenges, adjustments to campus life, celebrations of achievements, and their hopes for future opportunities. The powerful online blog also showcases the need for enhanced mental health awareness on university campuses.

Since its inception, *UNTOLD: The Campus Diaries* has grown globally, capturing the dramatic impact of student voices. Like other facets of the entire UNTOLD Project, the student's voice is heard through the art of both conversation and written word. It allows for unspoken and silent topics to be given a safe (and anonymous) place, free of judgment, where shared experiences help fellow students through their own hardships.

The project allows students not only to be heard but to foster education, hope, and compassion within the campus community as mental health issues are elevated.

The Campus Diaries project expanded in 2021 to showcase selected, anonymous student essays in a traveling exhibit that is displayed in high-traffic sites on campus. The UNTOLD team is currently partnering with universities to bring this exhibit to campuses around the world and positively impact mental health in student communities.

This book contains unedited entries by anonymous students. These authors' words and thoughts are unfiltered. We hope the original essays will create change within the hearts and minds of the students and across their host communities as we strive for enhanced mental health throughout society.

No one prepares you for the stress
that is about to unfold.

—Canadian University student

THE WEIGHT OF THE WORLD

Dear Diary,

    I've never felt this overwhelmed in my entire life. I oftentimes catch myself just lying on my bed, staring up at the ceiling, hoping that something new and good will happen. It never does. This is not what college is supposed to look like.

    I think about how last March I was so excited for classes to go online because it was a fun change in pace and aligned itself with my introverted self. In January, when I stepped onto campus for the first time in almost a year, I cried. I cried because, for one hour a week, I get to experience being on a college campus again. I cried because this is the last time I will ever be able to enjoy undergrad. I cried because I only have two more months left at school, and it's ending in such chaos.

    I shouldn't cry for things that are out of my control. I should also take my blessings where they come. I work from home, I do school from home, I have a good home, and I have friends and family around me. More often than not, though, I catch myself staring at that same exact spot on my ceiling, wishing for something different. I feel overwhelmed.

    I feel overwhelmed staring at my plants as they wilt over because I haven't watered them in weeks. I feel overwhelmed at the pit in my stomach because the thought of cooking sounds all too much. I feel overwhelmed at the dwindling stack of toilet paper in my linen closet because another trip to the store sounds exhausting.

    All I want to do is play my video games, but even that sounds too exhausting. I am overwhelmed by school. I am overwhelmed at the thought of doing anything of substance. I am overwhelmed at the idea of being a human again.

    I am overwhelmed with the weight of the world.

SOMETIMES LIFE THROWS ROCKS AT YOU

Dear Diary,

    This past academic year has possibly been my favorite during my three years at UF. I made new friends, got a good job, and grew less dependent on my boyfriend. The good things have outweighed the bad, but the bad has still been bad. I've dealt with anxiety, grieved a death, got placed into therapy (maybe a good thing?), and worked with a lazy boss who just yells at me half the time.

    However, this year, I joined an organization that transformed by college experience, and I'll always be grateful for all my brothers. They have no idea, but I was in a really low place before I met them all; and they have brought me out of that and taught me just how important friendship really is. This organization will define my college experience in all the best ways. I just made my friends last October; and now as graduation nears, many of them are leaving. It is sad because it reminds me how temporary life is; nothing is ever truly permanent. I worry that next year, my senior year at UF, won't be as enjoyable without the people graduating in a couple of weeks. I try to stay hopeful, and I am. I just hope I don't have to make a whole new set of friends. It was hard enough making these. Haha!

FINDING YOURSELF

Dear Diary,

I was a freshman in fall 2017. Now I am graduating in May 2021. That's fiftyish days from now. Let me just tell you a little bit about my college experience and how I have changed as a person.

Like I said, I came to MTSU in the fall of 2017. I was in the marching band, and I knew no one. That was because I came from out of town. But I made a couple of friends, and that semester was filled with going to football games and failing biology. I know. Sounds fun, right? I was exhausted by the time winter break rolled around. But once that first semester ended, I finally had a grip on how the college world worked.

That second semester of my freshman year was what defined and changed my college experience altogether. By doing what? You may ask. I joined a sorority here on campus. If you know me, that is sooo out of my comfort zone! But let me tell you something; I thrived! I absolutely had the time of my life in that sorority for two years! I held many leadership positions, my sister was the best they could be, and I felt that I had found a group of women who uplifted me and one another.

However, the spring semester of my junior year was when things started to go downhill. My sisters were becoming more detached from one another, and they fought constantly. The cycle was never ended. They would smile to your face and then talk about you behind your back. That was when I started to shut everyone out. I would pretend that I was still having fun, but on the inside, I was miserable! This group of women was going downhill fast. I still don't know what had changed from the previous semesters. Maybe they had spent too much time together? Maybe they truly didn't like each other and were just finally showing that for the first time? I don't know. But it began to affect me and make me feel things that I have never felt before.

The first semester of my senior year was awful. Because of the lonely feeling and terrible mental state, I became someone who was so angry at myself as well as all my sisters. I bullied them. I treated them terribly. I even made one girl cry because I had talked down to her and made her feel bad. That was because I wanted them to feel the pain they were causing me. I hung out with a group of sisters who were just awful people! Because of this, we were feared, and we made people feel uncomfortable. No one wanted to hang around us, and that hurt me on the inside. These women became my only friends. Because I had been mean to everyone, I shut them all out and never got to make any more friends besides these women. And that caused my mental health to decline even more.

These sisters that I hung around also were bullies, but I don't think they understand that to this day. They ended up dropping out of the sorority. I don't hang around them anymore, and I am so thankful I don't because they were never my true friends. They did not care what I did and never checked up on me if they did not hear from me for a while. They egged me on when I bullied another sister and laughed at every mean thing I said or did. That made me even more mean and rude to my other sisters because these certain women made me feel "cool" and "loved."

But that is not how a true friendship is supposed to work. True friends are supposed to tell you when you have gone too far and let you know that it is not okay to say these things to others. However, this group of women did not do that; in fact, they did the complete opposite. They bullied everyone right along with me. And when I noticed that, that was when I realized that I needed to get out of that friendship. I was hanging on to it because it was the only thing I had. I didn't want to let my only "friends" go, but in reality, the friendship between me and them had ended long before this semester. It just took me a while to come to terms with that. So I left the friend group even if that meant I had to spend the last semester in college alone. It was better than losing myself to people who never cared.

But you want to know what I realized? Letting them go and letting go their negative energy have changed me for the better. It has helped me understand that I have to take responsibility for my actions. It also showed me that friendships can be damaging and toxic as well, and it can turn you into someone you don't recognize.

I ended up apologizing to the sisters I bullied and made feel uncomfortable, and I have never had a friendship that was this uplifting. These new friends actually care about me, and they love me for who I am. They forgave me instantly for the way I treated them that semester. No matter what I said or how I acted, they began to love me and help me see my potential. They opened up their hearts and minds to me; and I couldn't be more grateful. That has strengthened our sisterhood and friendship, and that is the kind of friends you should have. By them forgiving me so easily, and putting their trust in me once again, that shows me the type of people they are—kind and courageous people—and that is who I aspire to be. These women showed me that being kind and honest will change my life and open up doors I never thought even existed.

This experience changed me from a cruel person to someone who is kind, someone who does not judge someone else as soon as they walk in the door, someone who opens their heart so that others can have a good experience and want to actually be my friend. (Do not let my story keep you from joining a sorority 'cause it will truly change your life.)

Overall, college is an emotional roller coaster that you cannot escape even if you tried. There will be many downs, but the ups that you have will overcome those downs and make the whole thing worth it. I hope that my story helps you understand that who you are and what you do will affect you and the others around you for the rest of your life. You may not think that you will go far in life, but just by being a good person and treating others with kindness, you will go farther than you ever thought was possible!

IS THIS NATURAL OR HEALTH ANXIETY?

Dear Diary,

　　I am not sure what I am facing. Is this natural anxiety or health anxiety I should be worried about? I feel all this emotion is a manifestation of these college changes and maybe even my own unhealthy lifestyle. It's college, right? So I am probably not eating right, drinking a little too much, along with other things I shouldn't be doing, and now my heart feels like it's going into rapid beats when I feel stressed. I struggle to focus, and I am really worried my roommate is unhappy with me. I feel like my heart is going to jump out anytime. These changes are tough, and I feel sometimes like I have chest tightness, and I might hyperventilate with all these changes, papers, reports due. It makes me very stressed and very irritable. I really want to make my family proud, so this pressure is probably on me. But I just don't want to fail. This isn't high school anymore for sure. I wish somehow the colleges would talk about the impact—huge impact—on the day-to-day health and well-being of students. Sometimes it's scary. Sometimes I feel alone even with lots of friends and lots of activities.

　　Anyway, for anyone out there who has stress, panic attacks, and scared, most everyone else is feeling it too. It may manifest in other ways, but the stress is real. We gotta hang in there. We gotta be strong. Just know, you're not alone.

I wish somehow the colleges would talk about the impact—huge impact—on the day-to-day health and well-being of students.

GUILTY FOR ENJOYING LIFE

Dear Diary,

    I constantly feel overwhelmed with schoolwork, and it seems like a never-ending list of things to do. When I do find the time to enjoy myself, I always seem to be feeling guilty. It is drilled into my mind that I always need to be productive and that if I don't do schoolwork, I will fall behind. As a result, whenever I take time for myself or spend time away from my computer, I'm constantly pushing away thoughts in the back of my mind telling me I need to be doing classwork. I'm so tired of feeling guilty for taking time for myself, and school has taken over everything I enjoy.

COVID FREAK

Dear Diary,

    This past year has been really hard between everything that has gone on, especially the pandemic. I have been trying my best to follow all of the precautions only for people who I thought I respected to tell me that it doesn't matter or constantly make excuses for their lack of concern. I made the decision to leave my job of several years because all I heard all day long was how masks don't work, the virus is no big deal, it's just the flu, the vaccine is dangerous, we can't trust the CDC, etc. The environment just became more toxic as the election closed in, and police brutality matters were discussed or really "dismissed." Between the new school adjustment stress and my toxic workplace, I was at my end and could tell it was draining my mental health. Though things have calmed down some, I still find myself bitter seeing people be so reckless on social media during a pandemic. I haven't been able to hug, go out to dinner, or just hang out with my friends for over a year now; but to everyone else, it's just another day. People constantly tell me I'm doing too much or that I'm a COVID freak, but I'm literally just following the guidelines that we're all supposed to be following. It's so draining being inside my house 24-7 for work/school, and I want to get back out just like everyone else, but I'm not willing to risk my or anyone else's safety to do so. I hope we can get back to normal soon so I can start liking people around me again, though I feel like I'll never forget their actions.

NOW I FINALLY HAVE HOPE

Dear Diary,

    I finally have hope. The stress with this election and the horrific behavior from so many (on both sides) has almost been too much to me while I am trying so hard to keep my head above water with staying safe and away from COVID, working, and getting my classwork done on time. I'm in my junior year, and I am really taking my classes seriously, but this craziness in this world has almost derailed my future hopes.

    Honestly, I am proud of America for standing up, getting up, and voting. I want to live in a country that people are proud of. We don't need divisiveness in society, we need hope. Today, I started to breathe again. The election is over. Now let's get this virus under control, get America healthy, get the world open, feel safe about congregating once again, get back to church in real person, and let's all get happy again. I have hopes today that one day, these may happen again. Let's stay in this together and love each other again.

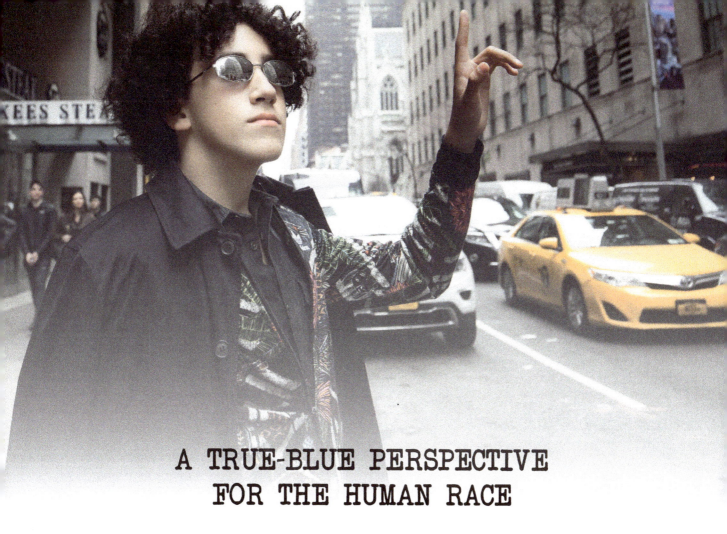

A TRUE-BLUE PERSPECTIVE FOR THE HUMAN RACE

Dear Diary,

    For one of my classes, I was asked how to avoid the dreaded Freshmen 15. After thinking about the topic for some time, I began to understand that I could not offer anything that had not already been said. Even if I had, I figured it would just come across, like the voice of the teacher on a *Peanuts* episode. I found I was at a loss until I redefined the question. I realized I was being asked to share my wisdom instead of my knowledge. Traditionally, students come to campus to gain knowledge. Being a nontraditional student, I have gained a lot of wisdom through the mistakes that I have made in life. Bad decisions come from a lack of wisdom just as much as a lack of knowledge. My nontraditional wisdom on how to avoid the dreaded Freshmen 15 throughout life: Make it a period each day and every day to interact with someone that does not look like you, does not dress like you, does not act like you, or does not talk like you. By doing so, you will begin to recognize that you have far more things in common than the things that divide and separate you.

ACCEPTANCE

Dear Diary,

    When the year 2020 began and news of the pandemic began to arise among media outlets, I initially thought that this would be an event of little consequence, at least within my life. I want to say that I later learned how wrong I was. But I think it would be unfair to say that I am finished with learning about both myself, both as an individual and of my life, during this time.

    As a former high school senior, I firsthand witnessed what it meant to have the idealized and long-awaited graduation be canceled, missing the opportunity to spend time with my classmates during what would be one of the most memorable nights of our lives, and not having one last summer with close friends before many of us would be heading into the next four years of both our education and careers. I recall saying that we would be seeing one another soon enough, perhaps during the breaks. But as we later learned, for many of us, that too would be one of the many things we had lost.

    You may ask, what does this have anything to do with perhaps a struggle I might have? The thing is, it was one of the main contributing factors to the growing issues that arose within and toward the end of the year.

    With the start of the summer break in 2020, I found myself diving deeper into books and questioning much of what I believed in, both spiritually and unspiritually, as a way to deal with having too much time on my hands. This curiosity later transformed itself into spiraling self-doubt after the fall semester. I started wondering, what if I was unable to perform academically well or if I did not meet the expectation that I have set for myself? Worst of all, what if I am unable to maintain the image of the seemingly perfect individual that I have cultivated and kept polished for as long as I can remember?

    I have personally heard from other individuals that being able to fail is okay. However, for me, I felt that this was never an option. When there are plenty of individuals, both in your family, your social group, and amongst your mentors that expect you to excel academically and be emotionally intact, it becomes harder and harder to juggle the two while actually dealing with conflicting emotions on the inside. The worst of this being, I wished that the issue resided on whether I could actually have the capabilities of excelling or getting good grades; but rather, the issue was the fact that there would always be an expectation that I work as hard as I have been doing for years. Perhaps today, it would be my education; but tomorrow, it will most likely translate to what type of job expectations and career ambitions I should have.

    I have pondered over what it would mean if I were to let go of all that and simply continue on with my life. But then I remember that it would mean disappointing many individuals who have been with me through much of my education and life. I still struggle with deciding between my happiness and my goals and aspirations to this day, but I have learned one of many things that I will disclose here: I will only get one life, and the opportunities that come my way are also the same in this manner. And while I may not know what the future holds for me in the upcoming years, I hope to be able to live up to the expectations and hopes of those I care about while finding a way to be happy and live the life that I envision for myself. All in all, the pandemic tore apart many of the dreams, goals, and hopes that individuals all around the world had. Though it may seem that the plights of this almost second-year college student may sound insignificant to those who lost jobs, homes, or family members, I want to say that I would completely understand such thoughts. Prior to the pandemic, I had never imagined that I would be one day questioning what to do with my life and the goals I have for myself. Yet I guess I find myself thankful for it as it has taught me one thing in particular, which is the following: that it is okay to have doubts about the present and future; it is ultimately up to us to determine what we make of these circumstances.

    I, for one, will continue to seek guidance and wisdom on how to proceed with my studies and career goals while determining what it is that I really want in my life.

OVERWHELMED

Dear Diary,

I have never struggled much in school before. This is my senior year, and I thought my last semester would be laid back and a time to make some last memories. While I am only taking twelve hours, I have never had this much outside work to do in my time in college. I work thirty-plus hours a week, and every other free moment is filled with homework, and yet I cannot ever catch up. There's always one class I have to let fall behind. I just have to keep rotating which one it is this week. It feels like the professors decided we had enough grace time during the pandemic and decided to amp it up one. I wish my last semester was one of joy with my friends and in my classes, but it's been difficult not to be frustrated at the amount of work I constantly have to do. I am grateful it's almost over and still grateful for the time I've had in college.

NONTRADITIONAL MOM TRYING TO MAKE IT WORK

Dear Diary,

I am a nontraditional student, I am a US Army veteran, I am a wife, and I am a mother. I am currently a senior at MTSU, studying photography. It has been tough to be a parent, spouse, and full-time student; then we throw COVID-19 into the mix. School has definitely been more difficult for someone who loves in-person learning and socializing. MTSU has done very well with accommodating everyone and making campus safer.

FOLLOW THE YELLOW BRICK ROAD

Dear Diary,

Follow the yellow brick road, they say. Well, I followed it. I completed my gen ed. I chose a major that I enjoyed. I picked the classes I wanted for the semester. I organized my schedule to fit my work/social life. I did everything I could to be prepared for this semester. Yet I still feel like I'm drowning. I haven't done anything fun or productive other than schoolwork for the last month. I feel like my days are on repeat—wake up, answer emails, sit in a Zoom call, do homework, study, work, sleep, repeat. I can't seem to escape this loop of torture. It's been one month into the semester, and I have already had seven (way too many) all-nighters just to hit deadlines. Even with all this work, my grades don't reflect the amount of effort I have put into these classes. Sometimes I just want to break. Although I don't know how I haven't yet. Maybe I don't want to let my parents down? Maybe I don't want to let myself down? I don't know. All I know is I have to finish out this semester. That's the goal, right? I don't even know anymore.

Send coffee.

AN OVERACHIEVER'S NIGHTMARE

Dear Diary,

    Each day of this semester has been a blur. Each day bleeds into the next, and I have lost all sense of control in my life. The student I was in January of 2020 and the student I am now are two different people.

    My January "self" had a planner, had a 4.0, was elegantly balancing work, school, and being president of her student organization, and most importantly, was happy. Today I find that I go through each day not knowing what will come the day after. I have no schedule, a half-empty planner that sits in my bag unopened, and a constant feeling of numbness. If not numbness, the only thing I feel is self-hatred because I have lost myself in the madness and am now failing three classes when I am supposed to be graduating in December.

I try to be kind to myself and rationalize my situation by saying, "You're living through a pandemic, you are struggling in isolation, and you are doing the best you can." But that's just not enough. I am an overachiever at heart. My self-worth is measured in my ability to accomplish things and accomplish things well. And now there is not a single area of my life where I feel that sense of accomplishment, not even in my personal relationships. Because of all the things constantly swirling around in my brain, I have detached myself from many of the people I love most, including breaking up with my boyfriend of two years. I've become a jerk to those who have shown me the most kindness in my life. I used to love college—every aspect. I loved walking to class, attending lectures, interacting with my professors, being involved in student organizations, and of course, the social life of it all. I could sit in the library for hours and be unfazed. But now, because of quarantine, my attention span has become so short that I am lucky to be able to make it through fifteen consecutive minutes of reading. I used to be admired for my leadership skills in my organization, but now I feel like all I ever do is drop the ball.

Throughout this semester, I have come to hate school. Every day, I dread opening my laptop and logging on to Zoom. I dread opening my textbooks. I dread planning meetings. It's all become so much. And while in the past I have been known for my ability to "do it all," I can't do much of anything now.

I just pray I'm successful every day. I think about my future a lot. I didn't come to college for nothing; and now it's time to grind even harder. I know life is hard, but I just pray to make it day by day.

LAST SEMESTER SURPRISES

Dear Diary,

During COVID-19 attempts to stay "safer at home," being mandated to work from home, and already attending classes online, I've come to realize I don't actually like my home. It took over six months of working at the dining table and being in a "funk" at work to accept I was depressed and need to change my surroundings. Work is crazy due to a large project. School seems manageable. I have only concentration classes left, and I've worked in the field for over ten years. Further, I took accelerated classes this spring and summer, and these are regular semester length. So I've added to the continuum of change by deciding to leave my partner of over 6.5 years and cultivate my own space (to include a DESK to work at). Though excited for the move, I'll be "homeless" for nearly a month, waiting on the apartment lease to begin. The business at work leaves me wondering if it's wise to immediately begin graduate school as I intended. I'm very busy but also very distracted.

I JUST WANT TO FEEL LIKE EVERYTHING'S NORMAL AGAIN

Dear Diary,

    I hate and love online classes. I originally took distance learning classes because of the need for work and life balance. It helps me with schedules, but it doesn't help with my social life. To be honest, I am a shy person, and I do not go out already. But COVID-19 is making it worse. I just wish there was a group chat where students could say a little something to cheer someone up, like a little "good morning!" or some random words of encouragement every day. I just feel like something needs to be changed about education overall though because the country is falling apart. The protests have brought a lot of attention to problems we have in society from racism to poverty, lack of programs to unemployment. I feel like we have to pay the most attention to education because it will help the country in the long run. I feel like fewer people are going to have the means to afford basic necessities, and we, as students, can't do anything about it. Tennessee is already very poor, and it's depressing seeing state representatives act immature and racist.

I just feel helpless. Last election, I could not even begin voting because I lived hours away from my residential address, and first-time voters have to vote at their home address, which I feel is a form of voter suppression of young people. It's disappointing to see so many immature and unprofessional people who exist in this country and especially those who are supposed to be "leaders." I just want to say that even though I voted this year, I still feel like everything is hopeless because America is going down the drain, and we have one of the poorest people even though we are supposed to be a developed country. And I feel like no one really understands anything and does not bother to learn basic facts about their own country. Overall, I just wish that we had better government programs and less corruption. But I am glad that since May, we learn more about who did what in the past, whether it was racist or something else.

It's not political to talk about general problems that have been going on in the country, and people need to accept that. We should talk more about these issues and work together to make changes in our state.

We need to band together like fan bases to get more influence on other people and the people outside our community so that more people in our government know that we want change. It's not about the people in power; students and teachers and citizens should have a say too. It's a basic right. I know I said before that I felt helpless, but I always try and be more positive. I think that we can still do something about the future. Let's all remember to vote. Let's fight for our basic rights, fight for more peace, and fight against corruption.

WILL IT END?

Dear Diary,

    I've been having anxiety attacks for a week now, almost every day. I've not really kept track ever since Mel's surgery on Thursday. Last Thursday was rough. Mel's surgery took six or seven hours. It felt like forever. Of course, it was the week I had to drive an hour each way to school. Thought about skipping, but I didn't. I needed the distraction. I also Zoom called a guy from Italian class, and we worked on an assignment together, which helped.

    By the evening though, when she was finally out of surgery, and I was home from school, I took a shot of fireball and was gonna watch some *Star Trek* to try and settle down. Within minutes of taking the shot, I got super disoriented and dizzy. It makes no sense for it to be the shot, but I didn't know what else to blame it on at the time. I was fine after sitting for a while and drinking water.

    Now when I try to do school, I get hot and tingly. I must be very deliberate about my breathing. It's almost like I forget sometimes. I have enough to deal with already.

I wish I didn't have to wake up every day to this war. All I've done for years is fight, and I'm so tired. Does it ever end?—fight for sanity, fight with Mom, fight for my health, fight for my friend's well-being, fight for my future and very life, and now just fighting for today. I want a break. I want to rest. I want to wake up and not be stressed and alone. I hung out with Ace and Will last night. I feel like I really click with them. It felt so good to be with people my own age who are also hurting. And nobody cares if someone else is a bit messed up because we all are. We're gonna hang out again sometime.

I guess I need to stop crying now and try to do school.

I'M GRADUATING NEXT WEEK!

Dear Diary,

  I'm graduating next week! I am super excited, nervous, anxious, and all the above, LOL. It's been four long, hard years. I've lost a couple of friends and made some even better ones. I tell you, nothing was worse than my junior year, but I survived it. I am beyond proud of myself and how far I've come. I've been involved on campus, I worked throughout my college years, and I've learned more about myself (what I like and dislike). I feel like my life is a movie sometimes. Graduating college is my greatest accomplishment because I never thought I would make it through college. I've doubted myself a lot, and at the same time, I have worked myself crazy.

  College is not for everyone, I can say that; but as long as you keep pushing, things will work out. The scariest thing about graduating is life after college. I have heard many people, some of them are my friends, talk about postgraduation depression. I am not ready for it, but I know it's coming. See, the thing about college is, they don't tell you that you're not guaranteed a job after you graduate. Some majors are, but most are not. Even with an internship, you're not guaranteed a spot. That sticks, right? That's the biggest thing I'm scared about. I don't have a job lined up. So what am I going to do? Another thing is, say I find a really good job, will it pay me enough? I never wanted to rush this moment, but now it is here. I am proud, but I am scared.

The way the system is set up, it doesn't make anything better. I'm one of those students that have taken out major loans just to go to school, so the thought of having to pay them back once I graduate worries me. What if I don't have enough? Then boom, financial crisis, debt, and I won't be able to buy a house, car, etc. due to poor credit. You see how this can become depressing really quick?

I just pray I'm successful every day. I think about my future a lot. I didn't come to college for nothing, and now it's time to grind even harder. I know life is hard, but I just pray to make it day by day.

MENTAL HEALTH AS A NURSING STUDENT

Dear Diary,

I am a senior in the college of nursing, and I am struggling this semester. Online lectures are hard. The extra work is driving me insane. I have three regular exams, three national exams, and four final skill checkoffs within the next 1.5 weeks! After that, I have Thanksgiving break then three final exams! Once I pass this semester (which I hopefully will), I will start applying for residency programs. However, I am so lost as to what type of nursing I want to go in. I have a little under two months to decide before I start applying. I do not even have time to think about the future as I am still trying to survive these last few weeks of school. How do I decide what to do with my life with half of my nursing school experience was spent online?

My mental health is deteriorating, and it's difficult to cope with the stress. How do I relieve my anxiety when my family and friends think I am being overdramatic since nursing is supposedly an "easy" major? I usually perform academically well, but these nursing courses are really bringing my GPA and self-esteem down. I know grades are not what makes a good nurse, but I want graduate school to be an option after working as an RN for a while.

I can only look at the present and do my best. I hope for a successful future in which I am happy to help patients improve their health.

DEALING WITH ANXIETY

Dear Diary,

    I am a senior at MTSU. I'm majoring in computer information systems and analytics. I feel like there is such a huge weight on me to be one of the first people in my family to get a degree but also not to disappoint myself. I often get very anxious with all that I have on my plate, and I know I shouldn't. But I just start stressing before I even get started. The crazy thing, I motivate people on my Instagram, and I release inspirational videos; yet I'm the one that feels empty. I feel like as a man—especially a black man. There's not many people I can voice this to. It just got bottled up inside me, and I just suppress it rather than talk about it. I know that is not healthy. I'm actually surprised I'm talking about it right now. I moved back home because of the pandemic, which is in Memphis, and I feel a huge feeling in my heart because I love being here with my family. But I know this is not where I want to be, and it's stressful when I think about pleasing my family but letting down myself and vice versa, pleasing myself and letting down my family. I can say a lot more, but I will stop there. Thanks.

I'M OKAY

Dear Diary,

    I've held it together for so long. Between school and working two jobs, I'm tired. But I also feel selfish and unappreciative for complaining because I'm blessed to have access to an education unlike many. I'm blessed for my parents. All at the same time, I'm tired and holding it all together for them. They worked hard to get me where I am now. As much as I want to give up, I can't. I know I can do it, but I'm tired. I feel like if someone were to ask me simply and genuinely, "How are you doing?" I would break down. But I'm okay. I'm also afraid for the future. I have hope that my degree will take me places, but there is still some fear and doubt that it won't. I want to be happy. I want to be successful.

THE BLUEPRINT

Dear Diary,

    When I was younger, I never appreciated the skin I was in. I grew up being teased about my complexion, and those things really got to me. However, as I grew older, I started to realize that my beauty doesn't necessarily have to be centered around my appearance. The way I treat others, and myself, is what truly makes me beautiful. However, my melamed skin puts the icing on the cake. To any other black woman reading this, know that you are beautiful inside and out. You are special and genuinely one of a kind. Always lift yourself up, and always be your biggest fan.
    From the diary of a happy Black woman.

REFLECTING

Dear Diary,

    TW[1]: disordered eating. It just started happening during quarantine. I was home all the time and gained weight. I've never been happy with myself even as a toddler. There was just no way for me to go to a gym, so cutting down on food seemed "rational." I don't want to say that completely because I know it's bad. I eat and weigh enough right now that I don't know if I even count, but I feel so guilty about eating outside of the limit or something that I can't put a number on. I'm sure others feel this way. I just needed to vent anonymously even if I'm not sure I count.

---

[1] Trigger warning.

IT'S A TIME TO HEAL

Dear Diary,

It's a time to heal. To hear those words from our first woman headed to the second-highest office in the land created so many emotions inside me. For the first time, I didn't just hear, but I FELT what a unification of a nation really could feel like, and it felt so good—so good, I cried.

What I have learned from this election is it's not about one person but about all people, a society—a society that loves, respects, and honors each other. It's about character, humbleness, hope, and true giving. That's what I was always told America was. I have not known what America was for some time. But tonight, this painful knot I have carried in my stomach for so long is now gone; and for that, I am thankful.

I have lived with my broken heart for too long. My heart hurt for so many felt they couldn't succeed. They didn't think they mattered or what they wanted to do would matter anymore. Some were wondering if being here at school was even worth it. No one would appreciate what they did. That seemed to be a new American mentality. But tonight changed my mind about who I am and what I can be for others.

For the last few years, I didn't feel I mattered. I was a nobody and, in the mind of society, might never be anybody. Tonight, I realize I do. Tonight, I realize I am. There's a shift in the air, and I love to breathe in this air of hope. Yes, there are others like me who care. I CAN ultimately make a difference. Yes, it is time for healing—all our healing. It's an amazing time to be in America and a beautiful time to have hope.

THIS YEAR HAS BEEN

Dear Diary,

    This year has been

        hectic,
        ever-changing,
        laborious,
        painful,
        laden,
        endless,
        scary,
        stressful.

    This year, as said by so many media reports, political and popular figures, friends, and family, has been "unprecedented." No one knows which way is up and which way is down. There is so much turmoil that sometimes I find it hard to breathe. I lost count of the number of panic attacks I've had this year—episodes that feel like my chest is trying to detach from my body—and my head is about to explode. I remember watching the news at the beginning of the year and passively dismissing the reports of a new pandemic that had been sweeping across countries like Italy and China. "That's so sad," I said to myself. "I hope that they can find a vaccine soon." Then the first reports of cases of this new virus reaching the United States were being splashed across the pages of newspapers and the screens of every major news network. I still didn't think much of it until spring break got extended. Then classes were moved online for the next month, then two months, then the rest of the semester.

    Quarantine happened. My husband worked from home. The virus spread. Masks and plastic gloves were worn, only to be tossed carelessly off the side of the road. What was going on? People started talking about the imminent apocalypse. God was finally seeking vengeance for all the wrongdoings caused by the human race.

    We deserved this.

    I was disappointed in humanity. Despite the governor passing a stay-at-home order, no one seemed to listen, and even less cared. I was frustrated, angry, and saddened by what was occurring. My mental health started taking a turn for the worse. I didn't know who to turn to because everyone seemed just as hopeless and confused as I was. Riots broke out as the Black Lives Matter movement took the country by storm. People were fighting for equal rights, while other people were fighting to keep the status quo. Violence, bigotry, and hatred took over, and the world turned into chaos. Then the clouds started to part just a little. Cases seemed to be going down, and the stay-at-home order was lifted. Some sort of peace was established, and the riots began to calm down. People started going back to work, restaurants and businesses opened up, and churches began in-person services again; but we all seemed to have an understanding that nothing would ever be the same. When we were finally allowed to go out in public, it was with the expectation that masks would be worn. These facial coverings took away something more than just our external appearance, they took away part of our identities. Smiles became less frequent, and true social interaction became a thing of the past. I began to wonder if things would ever change.

I started my final semester of school in August, which consisted of a teaching internship. I walked into the classroom on my first day, feeling as if I was in kindergarten all over again. The children came in, all wearing masks. They were seated on opposite sides of the table. Some of the students were only present virtually. I realized how much I missed seeing faces and how strange it must be for these kids to come back to school wearing new disguises. Even now, as we begin to wrap up the semester, I wonder what the long-term effects of this pandemic will have on this and future generations.

But there is hope.

I've seen so many people come together and join forces to fight this seemingly endless battle. Doctors, nurses, teachers, and other essential workers fought through the virus to provide services that we would not have been able to survive without. They risked their lives at the height of the pandemic to make sure that people were taken care of. When COVID-19 becomes a distant memory, you have my promise that I will remember you. I've seen the heroic efforts made by "ordinary" people who put their safety and health to the side to take care of loved ones. The country has united in ways that have not been seen since 9/11. And I've realized there is so much good to focus on. Yes, COVID-19 has made 2020 an endless cycle of confusion, stress, frustration, and fear. But I also know that everything will be okay. In August, I found out that I have a new life growing inside of me. What a symbolic and representation of a new beginning. I needed this. And as my baby continues to grow, so does my hope that we will come out of this stronger than ever before.

Yes, this year has been "unprecedented." We've fought, we've triumphed, we've laughed, we've cried. We grew tired, but we never surrendered. I have fought harder to stay positive this year more than any other year of my life. While there have been times that I wanted to crawl into my own private corner of the world, I knew that wouldn't be helping anyone or anything. When I couldn't persist and fight for myself, I persisted and fought for others. The year 2020 will be a year that no one will forget.

This year has been

> hopeful,
> encouraging,
> life-changing,
> purposeful,
> fierce,
> uplifting,
> laudable.

UNWANTED

Dear Diary,

How do you feel wanted? How do you feel not alone in a house full of people? I'm so overwhelmed between school, work, and taking kids to practices; but I still feel alone. I didn't think I would be getting a divorce after three years of marriage, but I am. Who would have known he married me for money, and that's it no support—nothing—just left with his two kids and a pile of bills. Some days I feel like giving up because, really, who is gonna want someone with kids in their thirties? So I'm forever gonna be alone. I don't like this life, and I would like to change it. But I can't. I just can't. Today was hard; tomorrow will be harder. I'm so lost in my head. It's not real anymore—just no one to talk to, and no one who cares. But then again, why would someone care? It's not their problem but mine.

I wish any that read this the will
to continue, to do your best, and to
know that you are not alone.

LIFE BEHIND A MASK

Dear Diary,

On Thursday, March 12, 2020, I was enjoying the end of my senior year. I felt pretty relaxed because I had a solid plan for college with some nice scholarships, and I was just having fun with friends and gliding through the end of my senior year. We had been hearing a little bit of a new virus though, but no one was really worried because it was all the way in China, and nothing like that would actually happen to us.

I was in my fourth period, coding class, when an unexpected announcement was made. We were told that due to the coronavirus, the school would be closed Friday through Monday for a deep clean. As soon as we all heard that, everyone erupted with cheers. We were so happy to get a long weekend and have some time off of school with little regard to the reason why. We were told that school would pick back up on the following Tuesday. But Tuesday never came. Over the weekend, there was a reported COVID case in our state, then our county, then my school. Things were becoming very real, although nothing felt real at all. Our state governor gave us a date that the schools would open back up, but it seemed like that date kept getting pushed back farther and farther. I didn't realize that the next time I would return to my school, I would be wearing my cap, gown, and mask.

On Thursday, no one knew that it would be the last day of school. I didn't know it would be the last time I would ever see some of my classmates. I didn't know that would be the last time I would ever walk around my high school as a teenager, as a student. A part of myself died that day.

Now the memory of the cheering in the halls haunts me. We were celebrating the very thing that was about to take over our lives. The next few months were rough. I never left the house or saw anyone because I didn't want to compromise my parents with whatever I was being exposed to especially my mom because she is at high risk with an immunocompromised disorder. I felt so alone, and it didn't help seeing my peers hanging out with friends, on the beach, or just looking happy on social media. I was always angry, anxious about the future, and depressed. Life felt like it was never going to move on from that point. It was almost as if time was paused, yet the seasons were changing, and life was moving forward in a twisted way. I selected two very close friends that I started to hang out with a lot, and my heart began to heal a little bit. I started to work on my passions, like piano, cooking, and origami. I was making progress, but the news of suicides always unraveled me, no matter how good I thought I was doing. Soon, the focus of my life shifted to college. It was time to sign up for classes and move out, and I was beyond ecstatic. This was what I was waiting for! This was what I had been preparing and working toward for so long! I was a bit naive and thought that as soon as college started, everything would return back to normal. But that wishful thinking led to many disappointments.

All of a sudden, I experienced blow after blow. (1) I am not able to register in person—time to learn how to use Zoom. (2) My dorm moved to single occupancy, which crushed my heart after I had been talking to my new roommate. (3) Only one class turned out to be on campus, and it was every other week. So (4) my parents and I made the hard choice to keep me at home. (5) There were very few activities to participate in because of my long commute and (6) most of them got canceled anyway. (7) I had to learn how to adjust to college while learning how to navigate remote classes. The course load word was so intense, and I felt like I was drowning. Then things started to look up a little bit when there was an advertisement for three girls looking for a fourth roommate! I checked out the place, and within a month, I was moved in. My parents and I decided it would be best for me to live here so that I can feel like a college student and be able to interact with kids my own age on a daily basis. I am so happy that I moved, but moving in the middle of a semester during a pandemic was very difficult. I had so many balls up in the air, and I accidentally dropped a couple along the way. I ended up dropping one course that I was not doing very well in, but I managed to keep up with my other four classes to remain a full-time student. Life is getting better, but it is still very difficult. I am trying to make new friends, but it is proving to be quite hard. I feel like a part of me has changed on an emotional level. I am craving friends and a relationship on an unhealthy level, but I am also pushing people away as soon as they get close to me. I am very vulnerable right now, but it is okay because I am trying to just take this one day at a time. No one could have predicted that this would be the reality of 2020, and I don't even believe it myself some days. Even though my brain knows that I am now a young adult in college, my soul is still waiting to go back to high school on Tuesday.

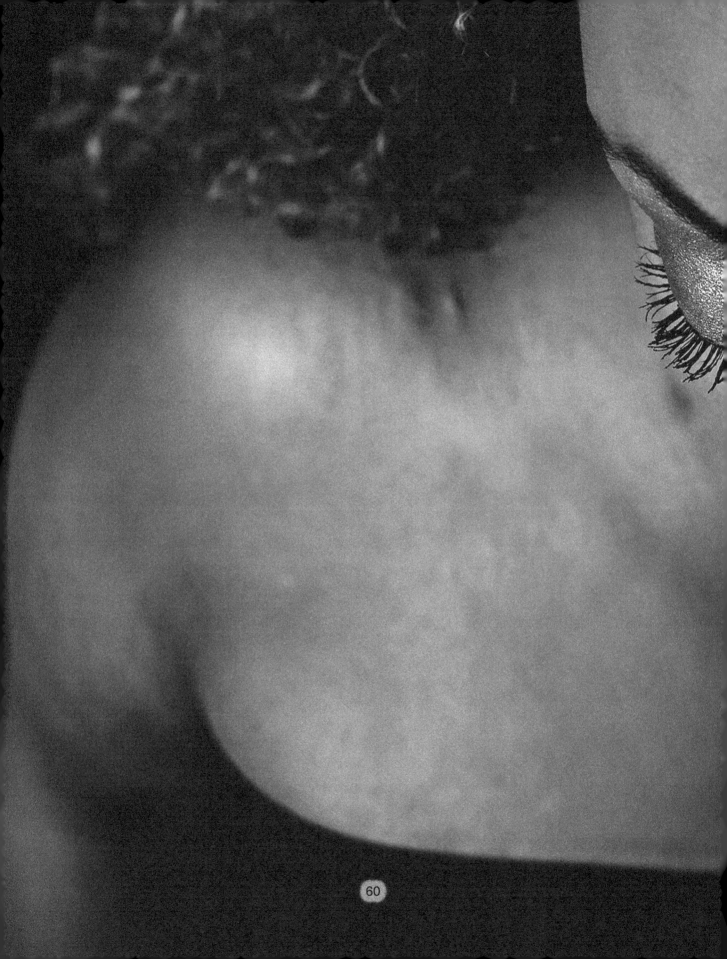

HIDDEN

Dear Diary,

 I've been contemplating about this for a while now, and I think it's time for me to come out. For majority of my life, I've kept this dark secret about being bisexual (well, at least what I think is dark), and now I am working on ways to come out.

 I know you all are probably thinking, *Just come out already, the world has changed.* But it is much deeper than that. LGBTQ gained rights not too long ago; and even 'til this day, we suffer hate crimes, injustices, etc. just for being the way we are and on top of being an African American, that is much worse. But let me get into my story.

 Ever since I was little, I knew I liked boys (DUH, of course I'm a girl), but I also discovered that I liked girls too. I had my first girl crush in fourth grade. I couldn't get enough of her, and I wanted to be with her. But at that time, girls being with girls was not right at all. So I had to hid it and sort of push those feelings away. There have been some girls that I have messed with, but nobody knows about it because I haven't come out, and the girls that I've messed with kept everything on the down low as well. I'm not going to lie, I feel ashamed that I have hidden who I truly am for so long, and I don't know how to come out. I've never actually been in a relationship with a girl, but I've messed with girls; and of course, those girls didn't want a relationship with me, and I didn't want to go public either. So why try to hide the whole thing? I told myself, when I came to college, I would come out, but I can't. It's something deeper within that won't let me be myself.

 My junior year, I was talking to this girl, and I really liked her; but I stopped talking to her because she was out, and I wasn't, and I was scared to get too attached. I know I need to be true with myself, but I am ashamed of that part of myself. I can tell you now say I come out today. So many people would talk about me, ask me questions, and who knows what else. Also, what would my family think? It's just so much that I think about that holds me back from being my true self. I know I want to get married one day, but I want it to be with a man. So am I really that into girls?

 IDK, I feel like it will take me to actually be with a girl to find out; but until then, I am still hidden.

SUFFOCATED GRAD

Dear Diary,

    Suffocated—that's probably the best word I could use that describes the way I feel. I'm constantly trying to better myself and my future with getting work done and finding new opportunities to do on campus. Yet it never feels enough. It never feels that I'm getting closer to accomplishing my dreams. I'm a first-generation graduate student. I come from an Asian American family where expectations to provide and to be successful financially are high. My degree has opportunities to expand in the field, but I feel limited with the area I'm in. Sometimes I worry about the future so much, I start to feel numb. I start to slowly drift into the idea of ending it all, including myself, just to stop feeling like a disappointment. I had plans to have goals reached when I turned twenty-five, and unfortunately, I haven't checked off half my list of what I wanted to achieve. I keep telling myself that my college and career journey shouldn't have a timeline, that my age shouldn't be seen as a burden. But how long will it take for me to feel like I can breathe again? I'm doing the best I can, but it never feels like enough.

THE NEVER-ENDING, BREAKNECK SPEED SEMESTER

Dear Diary,

During the summer, all I could think about was how much I wanted classes to begin. I had grown so bored of the monotony of quarantine and just wanted a hint of normalcy back in my life that returning to classwork and returning to my assistantship would bring.

But that normalcy never came.

Nothing about any of this is normal despite what the higher-ups are trying to convince us of. While I thought that I would be able to enjoy some parts of this semester, it has honestly been the hardest semester of grad school and of my academic career.

All of the professors, in an attempt to make things have some sense of normalcy, have overshot and are assigning an absurd amount of homework and projects. It feels as if there is absolutely no acknowledgment of the impact this global pandemic is having mentally on students apart from the occasional administrative email of "we're here for you."

I'm a 4.0 student, love to write and do research, and will happily throw myself into unknown realms of academia just for the experience. But how can I do this when my sheer existence, my right to life, liberty, and the pursuit of happiness are in question starting from the very top? It feels as though this semester will never end. But then I look at the unbelievable number of assignments I have due within three weeks, and I am reassured that this semester is coming to an end at breakneck speed.

I wish any that read this the will to continue, to do your best, and to know that you are not alone. If you do not do well this semester, that's okay. It's not your fault. You did everything you could, and that's enough.

You are enough.

UNCERTAIN

Dear Diary,

Where did this numbness suddenly come from? I was doing so well: keeping a consistent workout schedule, staying ahead of my schoolwork, having a pretty good body image.

But now, it all feels empty.

Workouts feel almost impossible to complete. Every assignment takes every ounce of my energy. My body is okay most of the time. Sometimes I feel so bloated, I want to pass out though. Sometimes I feel so numb, I think I will just pass out, that my body will cave in on itself, and I'll just fade into nothing. But maybe that's what I want. Every conversation takes so much effort, which only makes me feel worse because I think I'm being a bad friend, which doesn't help when you live with your friends. Because if I stayed in bed all day doing nothing, they'd probably notice, not like my mom. I often fantasize about what I would tell my therapist if I had one. I've done this for years because I always fantasized about getting help. I just had to wait until I turned eighteen. But then I turned eighteen, and I still didn't get help. Now I'm twenty, and I still haven't. I'm scared they'll tell me that I'm just normal, that I'm supposed to feel this way, that everyone feels this way, that I have no reason to feel this way. Maybe everyone does feel this way. Maybe we're all just shells of people walking around, pretending to have feelings.

Yesterday was pretty good during the radio show. I had a lot of fun. But then later that night, this feeling crept back up again uncertainty. I started doubting whether changing my major was really the right decision. Then I started wondering if media is even something I need to be doing or if anything is really what I want to be doing. On my way to work, I was thinking about whether college is really as useful as people say it is. What if I get out and can't find any jobs? I'm trying really hard to get experience, with WMTS or MT10, so that doesn't happen, but I also can't help feeling like that isn't enough. And then all my time spent at college will have been wasted. I want to try harder, but all I want to do is sleep all day. Every time I think, *This will be the day I skip this class.* But then I don't because anxiety tells me failure is the worst thing that can happen, which is good because it stops me from skipping class.

I'm just very stressed—stressed that my friends hate me, stressed that I'm not trying hard enough, stressed that my GPA will fall, and I'll lose all my scholarship and grant money. Really, none of these things are probably true. But I can't help but worry about them. All. Day. Maybe it's good for the most part because the fear of these things is what keeps me from completely giving up. But maybe it also isn't good because stress is the silent killer.

COLLEGE LIFE IN A PANDEMIC AFTER AGE THIRTY-FIVE

Dear Diary,

I started school back in January for the first time in almost eleven years. I am thirty-seven years old and a nontraditional student. I had already received my AAS from another college, and I was anticipating the college experience to be somewhat the same.

Boy, was I wrong.

It is so much different and difficult to go back when you are older. Also, being a single mom with teenage boys is a challenge alone. Don't get me wrong, I am grateful I am back in college and have waited a long time to do so. But like many, I did not expect a pandemic to hit and must become a "guinea pig" for this new way of college-life experience.

I am a very hands-on visual learner. Having to go remote strictly was a challenge in itself for me. I like to be in the classroom, I learn better that way. When you take online class by choice, you know that you have to be structured and more disciplined. This is a task for me not only keeping up; but if the interface does not work properly, or you cannot communicate with your professor effectively, it leaves a margin for huge misunderstanding and error.

I feel lost sometimes. I get frustrated. And I think to myself, this is supposed to be a good thing I have waited so long to finish. Why is it so hard? I know we have no control over the pandemic, and I try to tell myself, "One day at a time." I still get down and have anxiety and even get depressed because I feel I could be doing way better academically on campus rather than on remote and virtual learning. I was so happy to be able to return to campus this fall, but it is still limited. I also find it difficult in classes that use outside programs (i.e., Pearson for math). The teacher does not control the interface, and it is hard to explain issues at times that you are having. Also, a big obstacle I have encountered is the limited access to my professors. We have Zoom meeting options, but that is limited because there is only one professor and many students. I also feel that the lack of being in the classroom has taken away the ability to truly learn. What I mean by that is if I am working on an assignment or test, and I have questions, I do not have the immediate access to my professor for help or as I would if I was on campus.

I know we are all doing our best, and I commend my college on all they have done to adjust to this precedent time. I still get overwhelmed. I try to not let it get to me, but I am human after all. I will try and keep positive and keep pushing forward.

No matter the frustration, I will do this. So to whoever is out there, you are not alone. We are in this together! We will prevail if we do not go insane first!

WHAT HAPPENED?

Dear Diary,

    Today when I arrived for on campus, I noticed lawn chairs grouped together on the student union lawn. As I stared at those chairs, I envisioned people sitting, talking, and laughing. I looked away quickly because I knew that NO such thing was happening amidst the current pandemic. This reality made me sad. I wondered, why did they put those chairs there?—as a grim reminder that we couldn't use them!

FINDING A HOME

Dear Diary,

    I finally moved out of my mom's. I now live at my dad's, and it wasn't an easy move. My mom provided me with enough anxiety to last a lifetime. I packed up my stuff last Friday and left, and I feel like it was the best decision I have ever made. I can sit on the couch in peace. I don't have to be the parent for my little brother anymore, and finally, my needs come first now. It was a messy move. My mom thinks I hate her. I don't hate her, she is my mom. But the manipulation, tears me down as a person, making me feel like I can't do anything right. The words she chose to call me, all those things, I did hate. The more I read, I find out she's a narcissist and codependent, and she relied on me for so much. But I just wanted to be a teen and have fun and do my schoolwork. And now I finally have that. It's going to be rough for a little while, but I'm finally okay and happy and so thrilled to feel free. She can't hurt my feelings now; I feel stronger already and feel like no one can hurt me.

To any other black woman reading this, know that you are beautiful inside and out. You are special and genuinely one of a kind. Always lift yourself up, and always be your biggest fan.

SADNESS

Dear Diary,

    I'm trying so hard to reach my goals; and yet at every turn, it seems like the universe is determined to stop me. I know myself. I know that the longer I am here, the more burned out I will get, so I need to finish soon if I want to continue the career I've imagined for myself.

    I've done this before. I burned myself out last time. So when I finally graduated, I no longer wanted what I had imagined for myself. I was lost, aimless, wandering the world with no purpose.

    I've found another purpose, but I am not educated enough to reach it. So I came back. I'm getting the education needed, but I only have so long before the education will burn me out, and I will no longer have the future I imagined for myself that set me on this path. I tried to reach out, to get help; but at every turn, I was spurned away. No one seems able to help me. They say they want to help, but when I ask for help, I get crickets. I am ignored time and time again. So then I have to ask myself. Is this worth it? Is my future worth it? Or should I just give up and disappear into oblivion. I can feel the darkness encroaching into what light I have left in my life. I wish things could be different, but I've learned nothing will ever change. No one will help you, so you have to help yourself. You have to be strong in your own right to survive in the world because no one will help you or shield you. So am I strong enough to survive?

STUCK

Dear Diary,

So I am in a relationship with this guy, and it has been four months. (So everything is still pretty new.) At first, things were going really good. We spent a lot of time with each other, we traveled, and we even met each other's family (which both of our families love us together). We always talk about our future together and how we hope to get married. It used to make me so happy. But lately, it feels like things are going downhill.

I haven't been as happy lately because I feel like all we do is argue. I don't know what changed. Well, I do know what changed, but I thought he would understand since I am still in school, and he is not.

Ever since school started, I've been more busy with assignments, homework, etc. My boyfriend loves spending time with me and being around me, which is lovely because you don't come across men like that these days. But like I was saying, I've been busy, and I haven't been able to hang out with him as much as he wants. This is what has caused the arguments. I thought he would've understood because he was in school not too long ago, but he doesn't. He feels like since everything is online, why can't he be over while I'm doing my work? To myself, I am thinking, *Well maybe, because I wouldn't be able to concentrate.* I have told him this, but he still won't let up. Sometimes I feel like he is suffocating me with quality time. You have to be able to spend time apart, right? Isn't that healthy? I don't know. I just don't feel the same anymore because with all of our arguments, he has made me feel like I don't make time for him, which I do. It's just not as much as he wants.

Every day, I am praying and asking God what my next steps should be because I feel like he has shown me a couple of red flags. There have been more things that have happened, but I'm not going to explain them here. I'm just caught up because you take time to grow and get closer with someone, and now it feels like stuff is going down the drain. Don't get me wrong, he is a very great boyfriend, and he has done so much for me. I just don't know what to do. I hate feeling like I am stuck. I told him that I am going to do some thinking about what I want to do in regard to our relationship. I tell y'all, he has said some things that make me what to stick it through. But the other half of me is telling me to take a break until after I graduate. IDK. I just pray I make the right decision because half of me still wants the relationship, and half of me doesn't.

Pray for me please.

BETTER TOMORROW

Dear Diary,

    I may seem happy and that I have control over everything; but to be perfectly honest, I'm not. Although everything in my life is going in the direction I want it to, I feel like something is missing. Maybe myself?—I truly don't feel like myself. I feel like I'm just a blood vessel of a human going through the motions of life. I'm trying. Really, I am. It's hard going from what you've known all your life to something you have no control over. Life. Every day my mood changes. Happy. Sad. Confused. All the time, it gets overwhelming. On top of that, I have to deal with work, quizzes, homework, and my future. It's all jumbled together, but I am hoping for a better tomorrow.

THE SUFFERING AMBASSADOR FROM KNOXVILLE

Dear Diary,

    You know who I am. I'm the guy who was everywhere on campus. I'm the guy who LITERALLY spoke with over four thousand students in the span of five months, listening to all their stories. I attended nearly all of the campus events and made a jacket full of buttons. I became acquainted with all of the cliques and clubs. I ate lunch with someone I hadn't met every day. And if all that doesn't impress you, I even walked every inch of campus, from the PSB to the UP building and from the MEC to Greek row. Long story short, I loved immersing myself in my college community. It made me feel great about myself and helped me speed up my learning curve when studying psychology.

    Then COVID started to get really bad in February; and the next thing I know, everyone is being told to go home, stay inside mid-spring in March. I suffered for the first two weeks. Not being able to talk with and BE WITH people hurt emotionally, mentally, physically, and spiritually. So by the third week, I accepted my new reality and chose to make myself believe that I was okay with it. After a week, I did. I was fine not being social. To pass the time, I played video games and polished off my must-watch list. By the end of May, I was bored, sad, and lazy. But then something great happened! Some people I had met from campus started to DMed me, asking me to help motivate them since their last memory of me was when I was charismatic, energetic, magnetic, and far from pathetic. So I fixed my attitude and remembered my future goals because that feeling of being needed again was empowering. I completed my summer courses with As; revised my résumé; started applying for scholarships, intern/work programs, calling/FaceTiming friends, and so much more! I'm on top of things now! I'm on a roll, and I ain't gonna stop! But believe this—this pandemic is far from over, and the demands of carefulness are going to be a part of our daily lives for a while.

BIG DIFFERENCE BETWEEN WORRY AND CARE

Dear Diary,

Is there a difference between worrying about others and genuinely caring for them? Often, being a six-foot-three black man in America, I must be overly aware of my surroundings and unfortunately account for other people's biases while simply trying to live my God-given life.

For instance, I was hired as a US census enumerator for the 2020 decennial count. At orientation, the only identification we were given was a lanyard that has US Census Bureau on it, an identification card attached. We were given a single cardboard placard to paste on our windows. I thought to myself, *You expect me to drive door-to-door in rural Tennessee with only that?* My mother taught me, no one else will think about your safety, especially being a black man, in America. I have one life. "Sorry" or "I apologize" won't be enough for my mother (I am her only son) because some coward felt threatened by my skin color while never meeting or having a conversation with me!

I took matters into my own hands. I had a friend screen print me some shirts that said *US Census Bureau* in big, white letters on them. I went to the library, made copies of the cardboard paper, and had them laminated. Before every shift, I would have my T-shirt on (blueish color, like a sailor's uniform) so that if color was your focus you, should be able to spot this American blue before my skin tone. I would have laminated copies on both rear windows, the front windshield, and the rear! I can't count the amount of times I was told before I even got out of my car not to step another foot. I can't count the hateful, suspicious stares of people passing by, WORRYING about what I was doing without ever CARING for me. I had a guy pass me by three times. I was on a rural road with my flashers on, preparing for my next couple of visits. On his third approach, he rolled down the window and asked, "Can I help you?" as if I needed a reason to exist and as if he was blind and couldn't see the notices on my windows, the letters on my shirt, the lanyard around my neck! I've had a long day. He wasn't the first person to stare or make me feel uncomfortable for doing my job (a government one at that). My response was direct and without passiveness. I rolled down my window, looked him in the eyes, and told him, "No, you can help me by minding your business and stop WORRYING about others!" He then proceeded to tell me he was only "concerned" for me. I laughed as he pulled off his hurt feelings. I am no coward, and I am unafraid!

CARE or concern, as he stated, would have been him asking, "Are you okay?" "Do you need help?" "*Is everything alright?*" "*I've seen you with your flashers on. May I be of service to you?*" It wouldn't require him to drive around me three times, each time staring harder and harder. CARE would have stopped the first time. I say all this to say we, as human beings made in the image of God, should work every day to CARE for others and to worry about them less! The world, this country, would be a much better place!

AFRAID OF MOVING FORWARD

Dear Diary,

    I have a popular story that I've been posting for over three and a half years. People have been asking me to make printed copies and open an online store, and I have everything ready and in my room, but I'm just so scared to open the shop. I know it would be so easy, and I can handle the workload; but it's been two months, and I can't "will" myself to do it. I only have a few more years to get my art up providing a steady stream of income (even if it's only a little), but I keep thinking about getting a job with my business admin degree and living here forever; and I'm paralyzed with fear. I have everything ready, but I'm so afraid to start.

TSUNAMI SUNDAY

Dear Diary,

It is eight thirty on Sunday night. I am working on a homework for the upcoming week. My sixteen-year-old is sitting beside me, working on her schoolwork, and Sadie, the pit bull, is snoring softly behind me. The twelve-year-old is in the next room trying to catch a snooze, and my husband has turned in for the night.

Sunday nights are the hardest, I think. It is the night that the wave of everything from the week before crashes into me. What will the future look like given the gravity of the recent supreme court vacancy? Working on an ethics question, is the world ethical? Over two hundred people have died from the virus that my neighbors do not take seriously; how can they be so selfish? Breonna Taylor's story breaks my heart. That could have been my neighbor, my friend. What can I do? Am I just a bystander in the world? It is Sunday night that the world falls apart for me, and an odd fear settles in. I repeatedly tell myself to focus on the task at hand. I feel I am not cut out for this. Am I making a mistake? Is this the right path? I don't know anymore. The online classes are challenging; I have so much anxiety cutting in during our Zoom lectures. It's hard to ask questions to clarify the topics; my heart races.

Tomorrow, I will get up early and head to work where I do not feel safe. They sent someone to work from home last week. Was she sick? No one is saying anything. Should I confront my boss about this? My mom had a heart attack in the spring and is at serious risk of complications if she contracts COVID-19. She does her laundry at my house every other weekend. Should I tell her not to come over for a few weeks? I feel frozen. How do I move forward from here? This tsunami of thoughts and questions is racing, and I cannot focus on the work. Why can't I concentrate? Think I'll just go to bed now. Tomorrow is a new day.

WHEN IT RAINS, IT POURS

Dear Diary,

    Sometimes it really feels like bad things come in waves, and the waves can easily become tsunamis. The pandemic has been hard. The Black Lives [Matter] movement has been beautiful and necessary and tragic and horrifying to keep up with. The election is a disaster. These are all things we are going through together, and they are difficult. And then everyone has their own lives and struggles and challenges.

    Lately, I have been bombarded with bad news and anxiety. My dog of 1twelve years has been diagnosed with bone cancer. We have three to five months with her. She has been my best friend since I was thirteen. My heart is broken. I am engaged, and my fiancé's mother has moved from stage 3 to stage 4 of COPD. She called the other day to tell us she is scared that she is dying. She is an amazing, warm, and loving woman. It hurts to know she is afraid, and it hurts to watch her son be afraid for her.

    I am stuck in a job that asks too much of me. I took the job while I was on a gap semester with the promise it would be flexible enough to work with my schooling. I am constantly overwhelmed and pressed with deadlines that line up with school deadlines. I tried to quit last week. They said they would try to find compromise for me to stay. So far, nothing has changed, and I am still so anxious every day I go to work. They made me feel small when I told them I was overwhelmed. I look for a new job every weekend, but nothing pays enough or fits my class schedule. I am normally a strong and confident individual. Lately, I cry at least once a day.

JUST A LITTLE REMINDER

Dear Diary,

    You're worth it. I know things are hard; but one day, you'll look back at your hard days and smile because of how much things have changed. Have a good fall semester. ☺

AM I DROWNING OR FLOATING?

Dear Diary,

 In this time of returning to school after twenty-three years of being out and raising a family, I feel like I am barely keeping my head above water. Never in a million years did I think I would return to full-time coursework in a pandemic. I signed up for on campus classes, and I have ONE. The other four are a combination of Zoom and online versions. Geology is HARD when it's not in person. A lab is HARD when it is not in person. The learning curve has been huge, and there are days I feel like I will never make it. My saving grace is that EVERYONE is also experiencing this together—professors, students, families, communities…ALL of us! It is hard to wear a mask and study in a library. It is hard to be isolated from other students. This is all HARD. I will survive.

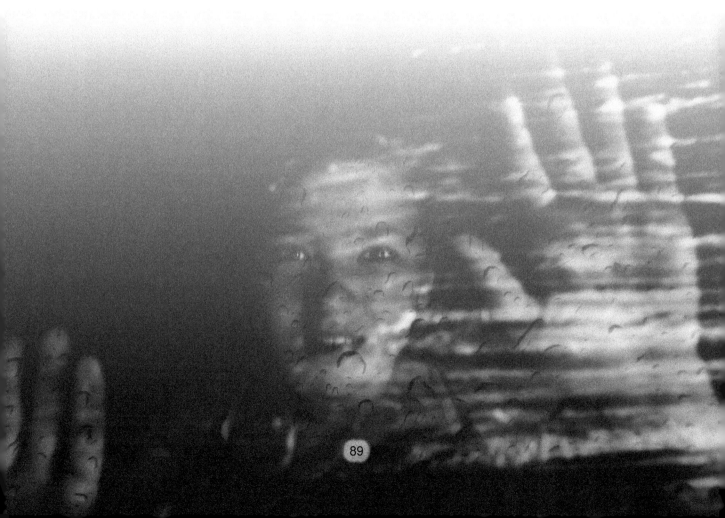

LONELY

Dear Diary,

 Ever since the beginning of this semester, I have not really talked to anyone. I don't have any friends on campus; I have no roommate; and if someone isn't in a group of friends, they kinda just stay away from everyone. I get that COVID is dangerous, and I take it seriously, but nothing is happening on campus where I can meet with someone. The most interaction I have had is in a Zoom class where we were discussing a group project. I want to join an organization or club, like maybe MT Lambda or something, but what's the point if no one is meeting? I'm just so lonely.

You are enough.

EVERYTHING I WANTED?

Dear Diary,

    I thought this is what I needed, to be independent and on my own. I thought that was the definition of thriving that I needed, but I didn't realize how much of an impact the pandemic would take on me. I thought spending all my time in my dorm would be great—all the alone time I could've wanted. But instead, I lay in bed staring at the same ceiling for seven hours on end, doing nothing but scrolling through my phone, wanting something to jolt me back to life. I feel isolated. Alone in a wicked way, I thought I would've been used to it by now. But something about being eighteen and alone sits differently with me. I feel the work I should be doing isn't getting done and overflowing on my desk. At the same time, an unsettling knot sticks to my throat, fueled by the fear that I won't do my absolute best. I have to be the same overachiever I was in high school. That motivation keeps me alive. It's six minutes 'til 9:00 p.m. as I glance over at the textbook with chapters I haven't read for my first exam on Monday. I feel like everyone from my hometown is doing better than I ever could, thriving without me in mind. I miss them, but I feel like I'm never on their mind; no one reaches out. But it's okay. I'll drown out my muddled anxieties with music for now.

LETTING OTHERS DOWN

Dear Diary,

    I feel like I'm letting my family and myself down. I would be considered lucky in times like these. I have a job that allows me to work from home, and I'm able to do a lot of my classes from home. But I still can't help the overwhelming anxiety and depression I'm having getting worse now that I barely leave the house. I'm starting to lose time, and a whole day will pass without me being present. I feel like I'm constantly behind in classes. I moved down to part-time at my job to help me out, and it made my mom angry. I think she's afraid I'll have to move back home again. Sometimes I'm afraid I'll have to move back home again. I've tried to reach out for therapy, but the ones in network aren't taking any new patients. It's getting harder and harder to keep my head above water, and I don't know how to tell someone without sounding like I'm being ungrateful.

I'M DRAINED

Dear Diary,

    I came to MTSU with the thought that I would finally have all the time in the world to do my homework and get good grades while also having time for friends and church. I've quickly found out that I only seem to have time for homework. Anytime I try to go do something for myself or even just go grocery shopping, my heart rate goes up, and I start to get really nervous and feel sick to my stomach because all I can think of is, "I'm losing time, and I'm not going to finish my work in time for class."

    I've made such amazing friends, and I want to spend time with them because I hate being alone; but I always get extremely anxious about it. I just constantly feel like I'm behind even when I'm not. I don't know what to do to cope either. All of the things I used to do that would help relieve my stress and anxiety suddenly don't help. I was at church the other night, having a great time, when all of the sudden, I just got this sinking feeling; and my chest began to hurt because all I could think of was the work I still had to do. I understand that you have to make sacrifices in college; but in all honesty, if I directed all of my attention to schoolwork, I would never get out. I probably wouldn't have made the friends I've made. I feel like it's a constant fight between "do I want to make good grades?" or "do I want to have human interaction?" Even if I tried to space it out, my brain couldn't take the fact that I know I have work that's due that isn't done.

    I have no idea what to do about it, and it's started to take a toll on my mental health. I'm too scared to talk to my teachers about it because all I can picture them saying is, "Figure it out or drop the class," which has honestly become very tempting; but I also don't want to disappoint my mom or lose my scholarship money. I just feel like I made such a bad decision with my course load, and I don't know what to do to remedy it. I'm becoming depressed, more irritable. My sleep schedule is messed up, my self-esteem has just gone down the rabbit hole, and I'm at a loss for what to do. I don't know where to turn because I feel like going to a therapist isn't going to help. I've tried to use a planner, but that hasn't worked well either. There are some times when I skip meals because I don't have time to step out of my dorm and go get food, or cooking will take up too much of my time that I need to focus on school. I understand that college is a lot harder than high school, but I think this is slightly ridiculous. I shouldn't be seriously considering dropping out because I feel like I'm not good enough or driven enough at least once a week. I just want to feel better about my schoolwork and myself. I'm so sick of being overwhelmed all the time.

COLLEGE IS SAD

Dear Diary,

    College is sad. Everything about it here is sad. The pandemic makes it worse. I'm stuck in my dorm and only go out to use the bathroom. I will not lie and say my mental health hasn't taken a toll in this either as my anxiety has worsened. I've found myself even being too scared to use the bathroom or to go to the SU and eat. I find myself deeply sighing after every Zoom class. It feels as if I'm not learning but just making sure I turn in an assignment before 11:59 p.m. I find myself crying every night because I feel like this was the wrong decision, the wrong major. Maybe I should've taken a gap year? Maybe I should drop out? No. I don't want to disappoint my family. It feels as if I'm getting this degree for them and not for me. If I do drop out, what's the other option? College has been shoved down my throat since pre-K; I know no other option. Now that I'm here, I hate it. I hate being isolated. I hate being depressed. I hate being so anxious. This is supposed to be the best time of my life, but it seems like it's the worst. Sleeping is the only time where I feel content.

GETTING UP WHEN I JUST WANT TO GIVE UP

Dear Diary,

    My life has been chaos, to say the least. I was homeless, my mother was a drug addict, I didn't know my father. I lost the only support system I ever had when I was fifteen, and I dated someone who was abusive. I know that I am not alone in living this kind of life. I have come a long way since fifteen. Yesterday was my birthday, and it had me thinking. There have been some days that I did not want to get out of bed—some days that the depression was so heavy, I couldn't breathe. The pain was so strong that I was walking across campus just hoping I'd get hit by a speeding car. At least the pain would be over, and I could just be done—done with paying for school, done with trying to keep up in class, done with this drowning feeling that was overriding my mind. But every day I got up. I got up, and I went on. And some days, it is still like that. I am married now, and I am in my master's degree. I just wanted to share in case anyone else has been in something similar and is struggling. I would love to say that this gets easier, but it really doesn't. Some days I do feel just as depressed. But I can say it does get better. Happiness is something that will come more often. Just don't give up. Get up, and face the day even if you only face it half awake.

To anyone reading this, I will be a graduate the next time you see me. Never give up! Crawl until you can walk, and walk until you can run to the finish line but never quit.

—US university student

11:59

Dear Diary,

I'm an adult now. I'm feeling like every day is the same—wake up, do homework, and sleep. Sometimes you forget to even eat. I now understand the saying ramen noddle becomes your best friend in college.

Sometimes you forget what day you're even on because life becomes the same routine. It's adult life. They say you're not a kid anymore. Your friends start to become strangers. You don't see them like you did every day in high school. But that's adulthood. All you need now is yourself. The only thing I could remember: 11:59. That's when your assignments are due.

Eleven fifty-nine becomes one of the most important things in life—a time that defines whether you lose or win in life. Are we even learning nowadays? When did school become more about submitted work than actually learning it? You get asked, "How's college?" You pause Zoom. When did school become more important than family? I ask myself. Grandpa was put on a ventilator a month ago, but you can't go see him. He's now coronavirus-free but still hasn't woken up. I forget what's even happening to him. Your family says, "You're not around, and you don't cry for him." When can I? I don't even have a single moment to breathe with my head all in books one subject to another. They tell you all you do is do schoolwork; you make it too big of a deal.

What can I say? Eleven fifty-nine is coming closer. I have to go.

LETTING GO WAS THE HARDEST PART

Dear Diary,

Until the age of seven, my life was pretty normal. I had a beautiful, vibrant family. My mother was a lovely stay-at-home mom, and my father was a navy pilot. We traveled all over the country. I felt loved, cared for, and safe. Somewhere along the line though, my family started to fall apart. Mom and Dad fought whenever they were together. And one day, without any real notice, he left.

In my teens, I would discover my father had filed for divorce before being called for a tour and wouldn't be home for a long time. It had been my mom's job to tell me what was happening. I didn't know it, but those were some of the last days of having a "normal" mom. She fell into a deep depression after my father left. I lived a dual life. I would leave my mom to go to school where I was happy, silly, and had many friends as well as made good grades; but when I came home, I became her caretaker. I would get off the bus and rush inside to find her still in bed, right where I had left her. I would feed her food and bring her water because I was sure she wasn't eating when I wasn't there. Things were really scary for a few weeks. Then all of a sudden, she was happy and bright, bouncing around the house, pulling everything out of the cupboards, and going on insane shopping sprees. She'd flit around the house from task to task, never really finishing any of them. For a while, it went on like this.

I felt everything was going to be okay despite the condition the house was in. Then she started going out all night and coming home intoxicated. She became very neglectful of me. I remember her coming home one night and making myself throw up so she would come upstairs and pay attention to me. Things took another turn for the worse as she again fell into a deep depression. After a few days of this, she woke me up in the middle of the night, shaking me, asking if my father ever hurt me. I told her no. She wailed and screamed as if I said yes then took me to the hospital. When the results came back that I was indeed telling the truth, my mother again screamed.

A social worker came in to ask if we had any family nearby to which my mother replied no. The social worker took me away and put me in foster care where, a few months down the road, my father picked me up. Confused, he asks what happened. I told him all that I knew. My dad listened with a sort of silence I'd never forget.

I didn't see my mom for over a year after that. I had no contact with her. My grandmother (my mom's mother) would call me and tell me my mom was doing fine, that we would be together soon, and everything would go back to normal.

I was almost nine before I saw my mother again. I saw her at the courthouse during the custody battle. I remember seeing her and feeling a sharp pain in my chest. She was so skinny; it terrified me. She was skin and bones and had a nose ring. Her hair was half bleached in a ponytail. She had on a thick layer of makeup. She kept smiling and waving and telling me she loved me. I told her I loved her too. As we left the courtroom, she begged me to come with her. She offered me toys—anything I wanted—but it wasn't my choice who to go with. I was to leave with my father.

This story has gone on long enough. You get the picture. It was an ugly custody battle, which by some miracle, my grandmother won. I wanted to live with her and my stepgrandfather in Texas. I asked my grandmother Meme where my mom went. Meme told me that she was in the hospital, "getting better," and she'd be out in a few months. I spoke on the phone with my mom once a week or so.

Eventually, my mom did come home. She was in a healthy weight, and things seemed well with her upstairs. It was finally clicking that my mom was having real mental issues, and it wasn't her fault. I remember after she came home, Meme suggested that my mom and I go on a date to the movies. So we went and ate afterward. I remember my mom holding up a jalapeño and saying, "Sweetheart, if you eat this, it'll show that you love me." I told her that I didn't like spicy food, that it hurt. She said, "You really don't love me, darling? I thought you loved your mom." She made a sad face, and I could see tears in her eyes. Out of guilt, I ate the jalapeño. It was awful, but she smiled and said, "Aww that's my baby! She really does love her mama!" and she laughed.

This may seem like an innocent enough situation, but I never forgot it. Moments like this happened a lot and, in the end, it was my mom's way of saying, "If you love me, you'll suffer for me." As time went on, my mother was allowed to take me to live with her. It was fine at first, but then I started to notice the same symptoms for my mom popping up again.

Her mental issues worsened, and the abuse began. Soon we had no food, and all things began missing in the house. I remember going over to my friend's house for a week, and when I came back, my home was trashed, and my Xbox was missing. My mom had barely noticed my absence. I forgave her over and over for her abuse. I honestly thought it all a part of a mother's love. I would always forgive her and say, "It's okay."

One of the greatest friends I have ever had in my teens looked at me one day when we were alone and said, "You know this isn't normal, right?" It started to click what was going on that day. I had been pretending to be handling it so well.

It all came to a halt when I turned eighteen, and I graduated high school. My Meme gave me a $500 check as a graduation present. My mom had my stepfather cash it at his work and tried to only give me $200 of the $500 gift. I called my Meme. My mom promptly gave the money back. My mom tried to say she was sorry, but I was done. For the first time, I told her this was not okay, and I was leaving.

That was my first step in letting go.

I moved to a city two hours away with my best friend. I became a traveling musician (technically, I was homeless for seven months) before I landed in Murfreesboro at the age of nineteen, going on twenty. It was the first time I felt truly free—no family, no background, no one knew me, a fresh start.

I had fun and got to know a lot of people and started school. All the while from afar, I would get random phone calls, updating me about my mom or random calls from random numbers from her saying she's doing okay but knowing she was manic. She would always demand forgiveness from me. She would always call and say how much she loves me. Eventually, a bitterness I didn't know I had risen from my chest and bubbled out of my lips when I was on the phone with her one day. I told her how she treated me was wrong and that she needed to get her act together and clean herself up. I let all of my repressed anger out on her that day.

I knew I shouldn't let hate and resentment bottle inside me. I decided to forgive her for myself. I realize that she's in such a tremendous amount of pain. I realize I love her, but I love myself more. I deserve to be happy. The hardest part was finally letting go of my past, of the pain, of the grudge. I'm unlearning all the manipulative, toxic traits I picked up from my childhood and learning how to love myself and stand up for my beliefs. Strange as it sounds, I'm glad for my upbringing because I'm that much stronger for it. I know I'll never be completely free of my mom. It's something I will forever carry with me. But sometimes, you just have to let it go.

TIRED

Dear Diary,

    If only the world could see my broken soul. If only I had the courage to speak out and tell the ones around me how much I am hurting, how I'm drowning. School was my way out. College was meant to get my life started and get me out of the constant tortious cycle I had become too accustomed to, letting others walk all over me and use me, taking care of everyone else but myself, letting my life slip right by me as everyone around me ignored my depression. I used to smile all the time. I bounce back, and people take advantage of that. But even though I felt so alone, I still smiled and pushed forward. Finally, I decided to push back and make life happen for me. I wanted to change the fact that I saw no future for myself, and college was how I was going to do it. I am visually impaired. And even though I could not afford college personally, there were many programs and things that could help me get started on this new path I chose for myself. I was just proud I chose to pull myself out of the cycle of nothingness my life had become.

    Before my first semester, my grandfather was diagnosed with stage 4 cancer. My grandparents raised me. They were my parents—so what a start to my new beginning. I struggled with that fact as I tried to make it through my first semester. I had lost more vision through the very same semester, making things much harder on me, and dealing with people who were mean about the devices I needed to use to get by. I thought college would be different than high school, and bullying would no longer be a thing. In the end, it's on me for saying nothing. But it was my first semester, I knew no one, and my world was falling apart. I managed to get past fall semester to go to spring. My grandfather was in the hospital my first day of class. I got the text, and I was breaking, trying to get through classes. He died by the end of January, never getting out of the hospital, and his last words when they put him in hospice being "they brought me here to die." Instead of dealing with his death, I pushed away from it, distracting myself with whatever I could. I started failing classes. My smile was fading. I could not find the strength to bounce back. I was more broken than I had ever been. I dropped all my classes but one. COVID doesn't help anything. It took away the one piece of kind I had—the job I had on campus with people who gave me light and a way to keep fighting. I found myself trying less and less and falling deep into darkness. When summer classes came around, I was barely myself. Only two classes and I still had to drop; one and the other one, I still failed. My self-esteem kept dropping. I let myself become numb.

    Now here is fall again. I'm still broken. I'm still lost. I'm trying but failing at classes, and I will lose my funding if I can't get my grades up. I don't know how I will make it without school. It's all I have left that's holding me together. I never got the chance to make some real friends. I know it's my fault for being where I am now, letting myself get to a fair place that I am still unsure of how to get out of. I just about lost all my fight. Without school, I have nothing. I'm trying to pull myself together. I'm trying to feel my loss. It only breaks me more. I need trying to be enough, but it's not. I need school. I need the interaction. I can't go back to being by myself. I don't want to. I'm at my darkest. My broken heart wants to cry; my numbed body won't let it.

NUMB

Dear Diary,

    Sometimes I feel like I'm numb. It's like I feel so many things at once that my brain short-circuits, and then I can't feel anything at all. When I'm not numb, I'm overwhelmed with all the emotions I try not to allow myself to feel—depression, anxiety, self-loathing, disappointment. I can't take pride in my work at school or at my job.

    My parents are divorcing after initially separating and getting back together ten years ago. My family is currently in the middle of our own civil war with brother against mother against sister against father. About three years ago, I was diagnosed with multiple sclerosis. I lost vision in my left eye for a whole week. I get infusions every six months to deter flare-ups that can cause my health to worsen. As of right now, I will never be cured of this disease. This diagnosis has made my mental and physical health declined greatly over the years. Freshman year of college, I wanted to take my own life. I had to go to a partial hospitalization program during my Christmas break. I'm no longer suicidal, but I do have bad days sometimes. I've struggled with my weight my whole life. I've never loved or even felt comfortable with my body. My weight, coupled with my disease and homelife, makes me wonder if I'll ever be able to find self-love or self-worth. I've tried therapy in the past, but I feel like I'm too busy to start back up again. I just want to feel like a person again, someone who deserves love and happiness and success. I often wonder if I'll ever get to that place. In the meantime, I think I'm stuck feeling numb.

UNRELATABLE

Dear Diary,

    I am a veteran and a nontraditional student. During my time as a student, I have felt isolation and an inability to relate with my classmates, especially traditional students. I have had some truly bad days, like working twenty-one hours straight outside in one-hundred-plus-degree heat because of a bomb threat—a bomb me and my team found. So I can't relate to your stressful day of having three things that are due on the same day. I try to empathize, but a lot of my emotions were beaten out of me by the military-industrial complex. I'm suffering from PTSD and depression. When I feel terrible, like I can't get out of bed, I still show up to class—because "mission first." My feelings didn't matter for years, so why should they now?

THE TEACHER

Dear Diary,

So there was once a teacher—no, don't worry. This is not THAT kind of story about a teacher, so hang with me. Look, I know this is supposed to be a "Dear Diary" kind of entry, but I just want people to hear me.

Several years ago, there was a certain teacher in my high school. This teacher wasn't like other teachers I have had throughout my education. Most of those were the educational-book type of teachers. But this teacher was a teacher who believed equally in life lessons as much as book lessons, and she helped me to prepare for where I am today.

What I have learned in my last couple of years, especially since COVID and all the ups and downs of life in the past eight months, is that college can't be all about books and tests. This world called "real life" and learning how to live and cope with life experiences along the way is probably the most valuable lesson I have learned so far. I am not the best student at ETSU by far, but that hasn't really mattered. Watching other people my age and in my class struggle with real-life chaos while balancing grades and responsibilities has made me appreciate those educators who believed in their students and encouraged them along the way. For that, I am thankful. So no, this isn't really a "Dear Diary," but I do want to let any educator, whether you are high school, professor, or doctor, know you are appreciated and to hang in there. We really are all in this together. And to the teacher years ago that showed me she really cared, hey, thanks. You did make a difference, and I am still doing okay in English—sort of.

NOTE TO YOU

Dear Diary,

    Know that you are beautiful and know you're worth. Don't let other people's words bring you down. Don't ever feel like you don't matter because you were the crown. You are a queen. Don't ever let anyone treat you like you're not. Look in the mirror, and love what you see. In fact, repeat after me: I AM BEAUTIFUL, I AM STRONG, I AM IMPORTANT, I AM SMART, I AM BRAVE, I AM FEARFULLY AND WONDERFULLY MADE, I AM GOD'S CHILD. I want you to keep pushing and never give up. You have a purpose on this earth. You are never alone because God is always with you. Be kind and gentle to yourself, and treat others with the same respect. Share your light. And remember, spreading love goes a long way.

LONELINESS

Dear Diary,

    Sometimes I feel so alone in this world. I feel like people always ignore me. I'm that person in the group chat whose message always gets overlooked. It's hard because it makes me not want to talk to anyone and to stop reaching out. But something deep inside me won't let me do that. I am grateful for my inner voice that helps me to stay positive, but sometimes I wonder how long that will be. I feel like no one ever really checks up on me when I always try to check up on others. Don't get me wrong. I love hearing that my friends are doing great, but I wonder how long it will take for them to check on me.

    Growing up, I was taught to treat others how you want to be treated, but I don't ever feel like that applies to me. Maybe it's something deeper that I'm not understanding. Maybe I expect a lot. But what's wrong with wanting to feel appreciated? I don't know. I guess, deep down inside, I don't really feel appreciated by people, and I try to push my feelings under the rug. For instance, I remember one time, I stopped talking in my friends' group chat for a month just to see who would notice; and guess who did? Nobody. I've thought about bringing it up a couple of times, but I feel it'll just get ignored. So, hey, what can you do? I just want to feel appreciated and not alone in this cold world. Is that too much to ask for?

STUCK ON YOU

Dear Diary,

    To the guy I still have feelings for: It hurts me that I still love you even after all you put me through.

    I don't know what it is about you, but I can't seem to get enough of you. I feel like stupid. I try to stay away because every time you're around, you seem to bring me back—back closer to you. I don't want it to be like that. I'm not even sure if you love me. And honestly, I don't know what this is. I imagined love to be different. Maybe it is. It doesn't make sense. After all these years, I still have feelings for you. It brings me to tears because I don't think I'll ever get over you. No matter how hard I try or what I do, I still think about you.

FOR THE BETTER

Dear Diary,

    Life is very overwhelming. While I'm glad I moved up here to seek independence, it's not working out like I thought it would. People I knew I'd be friends with forever no longer speak to me. I can't find a job. I hate online courses. I don't know my purpose or why I'm here. And the worst part about it is that none of this is in my control. All I can do is keep looking for work and keep pushing these classes. It feels very lonely. While I understand God puts us through seasons, I'm tired of them. I want stability in my life for once. But again, it's not in my control. While I keep thinking all of this is for me to grow, I don't know what I'm growing into. As a person who can't stand not knowing the answer to everything, I'm very uncomfortable. I guess I'll just have to pray that it all works out for the better.

THE QUEEN I AM

Dear Diary,

    Although this is old news, I would like to share this. I don't know why this has been on my mind lately, but I am thinking about a past relationship that I had coming into college the first semester of my freshman year.

    I was in this relationship for almost a year. At first, everything was great. He was a nice guy, really sweet, handsome, and he loved spending time with me. It wasn't until the sixth or seventh month when I started to see his true colors. I remember when he started tripping on me and telling me that I couldn't hang with my friends. He told me that he felt like they weren't good for me. He thought that when I hung out with my friends, they would influence me to sneak around, which was never the case. He always wanted me in his sight. I stayed around him 24-7, just sitting at his house, watching TV with him, or at his friend's house with him, watching them play the game. At the time, I didn't think anything of it. I actually enjoyed spending time with him and his friends because I was friends with them too. Now that I look back on that relationship, we hardly went anywhere or on any dates, so I don't know why I stuck around for so long. Also, he never bought me anything during Christmastime when I got him a nice amount of stuff.

When I came to college, that was when it really got bad. I remember the day I moved in. That following night, he wanted to FaceTime; so of course, I did. We had a good conversation for the most part. We stayed on the phone until we both went to sleep. Throughout the night, the call dropped. When I woke up the next morning, he blew my phone up, asking me why I hung up, what was I doing, etc. He tried to accuse me of cheating and several times after that. I never went anywhere the first semester of my freshman year because I didn't want him thinking I was doing stuff. I went straight to class and back to my dorm. I sacrificed my fun. I never understood it. I don't know why I continued to stick around through that. I remember he started saying I was boring and that I didn't know how to have a conversation. He always talked down on me. It wasn't until the tenth month that I decided that I had enough of his toxic ways. I was tired mentally and emotionally. At this point, I became numb to everything. I finally told him off. I was sad at first, but I honestly couldn't do it anymore. I was tired of crying, downing myself, feeling alone, etc. From that day on, I promised myself I WOULD NEVER settle for less; and that goes with any- and everything. Never let a guy belittle you and make you feel worthless. About two to three months after that relationship, I found out he was the one that was cheating on me—crazy world, right? It took me four years to be able to be in another relationship again, but I don't regret waiting. I am happy now, I know what I deserve, and I have someone that treats me like the QUEEN that I am.

WE WILL MAKE IT THROUGH

Dear Diary,

    I just want to start by saying we will make it through this together. There are so many things going on in today's world that are sort of out of our control. I have been taking this time to enjoy what is taking place. I have been looking at the good coming out of this situation—praying, exercising, doing schoolwork, spending time with my loved ones, etc. These are the many activities that I've been doing every day and enjoying. Do what makes you happy even if you can't go somewhere. Use this time to really focus on you and who you are as an individual. Get closer to your loved ones. Get closer to God. I like to always make the best of every situation, and that is exactly what I'm doing. We will make it through this, guys. Check on your loved ones and better yourself. Stay blessed, and keep the faith!

A DATE WITH ANXIETY

Dear Diary,

    Since the beginning of March, I feel like I've been in a serious and committed relationship with anxiety. Most nights, I have an anxiety attack in my sleep, and they have gotten better over this time period but still plague me. Schoolwork and everything all wrapped into one takes over my mind. I continuously pray and talk to God about life and what is best for me within my future. Everything that is going on in the world currently does not help my anxiety-prone mentality. I choose to take at least thirty minutes out of each day to write my feelings out and somehow declutter my mind. I have the highest hopes for the year or 2020 postquarantine and the greatest belief that I can get a handle on my anxiety and everything that causes me to worry.

NOBODY KNEW

Dear Diary,

    The seasons changed. And so did my mood. I felt sad a lot more than usual. My classes were difficult, and trying to balance everything ultimately began to take a toll. It went from missing classes here and there to not eating, from not eating to just staying in the bed all day. When I did go to class, it was like everything was in one ear and out the other. Ultimately, it reflected in my grades, and I got to a really dark place. And I never spoke about it. Nobody knew. Seasonal depression is real, and the signs are always there if you pay enough attention. But don't suffer alone, speak up. Tell somebody. Because suffering in silence kills more in you than anybody would ever know. Someone cares, and you are not alone.

LIFE

Dear Diary,

    Sometimes, when I think back on how far I've come from where I started, I'm in awe. Growing up with my mother and sister, things weren't always necessarily easy. However, I'm a strong believer in everything happens for a reason. Throughout my life, I have met some people that I will forever hold dear to my heart—those who have encouraged me, pushed me, loved me all the while, allowing me to be myself. To graduate college is only a dream to some. I'm thankful to have had a good support system through my college days.
    College will forever hold some of the best days of my life.

TRUST

Dear Diary,

    Last semester, I struggled mentally, emotionally—you name it. I wasn't succeeding in school like I should've been or, rather, like I've always done. It's like everything hit me at once. I was at a low point. However, in the midst of all of my downs, there's one person I knew I could always turn to who is never failing, and that's the Lord my Savior. I'm getting better every day at giving my problems to Him and leaving them there; and it's made me feel so much better or, rather, refreshed.

The Lord is my strength and my shield; in him my heart trusts, and I am helped; my heart exults, and with my song, I give thanks to him.

—Psalm 28:7

COMING HOME

Dear Diary,

    I love being at school more than the average student. Every aspect of college life excites me from being able to be around like-minded peers to learning from professors in class. Coming to college and being on my own have allowed me to feel freedom for the first time in my life with little to no restrictions. I'm able to do what I want when I want without the worries of what my parents think. Due to the uprising of the coronavirus (COVID-19), I've been forced to move back home, and I feel as if it's all been taken away. I don't get to see my peers anymore, and I'm back to following my parent's rules. It's depressing at times and makes me feel as if my freedom has been stolen. It's been a very challenging time mentally to adapt to being under my parent's oppressive ways of thinking, but I'm taking it day by day. I'm sure I'll get through this, and life will be back to normal in no time. I just have to stay strong.

I'M STILL HERE

Dear Diary,

For years, I have lived with mental illness. When I was sixteen, I was diagnosed with moderate depression. But really, what sixteen-year-old COULDN'T be diagnosed with that? The pressure to be beautiful and perfect is far heavier than any weight I've tipped the scale at; and while I have become more comfortable in my own skin, I still battle those feelings of worthlessness EVERY. SINGLE. DAY.

There was a time when the only relief I felt was watching a line of bright red blood appears on my arm, following the deep drag of a razor I had taken apart. It's been years since I've hidden myself away to cut, but the thought remains constant.

I have never told my professors. I have pressed forward, pretending everything was all right, that the things I had experienced to bring me to this place were not going to break me down, leaving me in a million little pieces on the dorm floor. You see, I have to remain strong and confident because I realized I needed me, and I needed to let go and get the help I so desperately wanted but didn't know how to ask for. So I did just that, and it changed my life.

GRIEF

Dear Diary,

    Last fall, one of my closest friends passed away in a tragic accident. He was my brother. I considered him a family member. I was closer to him than my own biological brother. When he passed, it was a pain I never experienced before. I never felt so angry and so hurt in my life. A wonderful person was no longer in my life. Even though I had lost numerous family members before, I had never experienced such a close loss like this. My friends took it pretty hard as well; and through it all, we have helped each other progress, but that still does not mean it is not hard.

    The stages of grief are very real, and I have allowed myself to go through them. I have also softened my heart toward God. For the longest, I was angry at him for taking my brother away. It is not easy, but every day, I push through. I cherish all the memories, videos, and pictures dear to my heart. His spirit continues to live on, and he will always be missed. He taught me that two and a half years can equal a lifetime. I thank God that I was allowed to meet such a wonderful brother like him. Hopefully, my testimony can let someone know that they are not alone, and you can overcome grief by going through it.

Be open and honest with yourself and the people around you. Don't give up. Don't ever give up.

DEALING WITH MY DEMONS

Dear Diary,

I am full again. The shame of my addiction eats at me like the ravenous beast who controls my mind. I stick my fingers down my throat and surrender to my demons. I feel so weak as I force myself back up. My demons are in the mirror, looking back at me. They dare me to fight back as they hide themselves from below the surface. No one knows what I am going through.

Bulimia, for me, is a form of negative control that started at the age of sixteen. My world was falling apart all around me, and the only thing I had control over was my diet and nutrition. Somehow, I lost myself along the way.

It wasn't until I was in my first year of classes that my demons reared their ugly heads. This is when they truly started to take control over my life. Being away from home for the first time was almost too overwhelming. So many changes and experiences, as well as having to deal with the expectations and pressures, I put on myself.

The good news is I realized I needed help, and I did start seeing a counselor. I was honest with them, and they gave me tools to help guide me to a path where I would slowly learn how to deal with my addiction. My demons don't define my worth anymore. I know now there is hope, and I am learning to love myself again. But every day is still a challenge.

Take my advice: Be open and honest with yourself and the people around you. Don't give up. Don't ever give up.

INSOMNIA

Dear Diary,

    It gets hard to read after a while—ya know, when you've done way too much homework for one day, and you have a couple of more questions to answer before you can wrap it up—but you just can't do it. It's like your eyes are doing pull-ups. And they thought they could only do three, but they're at five. And if they try to do any more, their arms might fall off. You were on your last leg an hour ago, and now you're done, tapped out. So you try to lie down and finally get the sleep you need. But what about that test tomorrow or that essay on Wednesday or the speech that you tried to get your other group member to do, but they had work, so you decided you'll just take it on, except its due by the end of the week, and you have absolutely no time to even start it, much less actually give it? No, there is no chance of sleep tonight. Instead, you're staring at your dorm ceiling, paralyzed by responsibility, smothered by your own thoughts and expectations and completely doomed to sleep at a decent hour. That is me every single night.

THE MOST BEAUTIFUL SMILE

Dear Diary,

 The war will be won. We visualize it daily while enclosed in our homes, isolated from peers of past, present, and future. You see, this war began far before any pandemic. It's the battle you and I fight daily on two separate battlefields. It's wild that we have to look in the reflective glass every morning and overcome that person on the other side now more than ever. You and I will raise our banners high one day, showing that we've won. We'll share our strategy with the world. The joy of overcoming really does bring the most beautiful smile.

MY COLLEGE EXPERIENCE SO FAR

Dear Diary,

    Since I started school, things have been different but in a good way. It has helped me grow and become a better version of myself. Keeping up with my schoolwork and going to work every week did seem like a challenge in the beginning, but I am making a balance. Also, having a support system is important. I have had my fair share of highs and lows like any other person. Even some of the people I have met are the reason I strive to achieve my goals and push myself to keep going no matter the obstacle. Some days I don't feel like doing anything, but I still manage to try my best to stay positive.

WILL I REACH MY DESTINY?

Dear Diary,

What has the world come to? It seems as if 2020 was supposed to be the year to refocus our vision. But everyone is blinded, not knowing what the future may entail. All we can do is pray to the man above that everything will be okay. I've got to admit, this is a scary time, making it hard to walk by faith. Hopefully, we can have the opportunity to reach our destiny. Do you know yours?

THE INVISIBLE

Dear Diary,

    I walk around campus, and I see faces—faces of people who appear to have it all together, who are doing well in school, and who have lots of friends. As I sit at home during this time of self-isolation, I scroll through social media and see the same thing. I have pushed everyone away. I have chosen to fight on my own. But the weight of it has become too much to bear. Each day, I wake up and feel unmotivated and purposeless; it's as if my life has lost all meaning. I only talk to one person each day. I have at least one hundred unread text messages from people because I'm too mentally exhausted to pick up my phone, or I'm too afraid that I won't be enough for them. It seems like everywhere I go, a cloud of depression hovers over my head and taunts me. It tells me there's no point in even trying because I'll end up being a failure in the end. It tells me how I'm lonely and how no one will want anything to do with the anxious, depressed girl. Some days, it tells me that there's no point in living. These are the things that people don't see. This is my invisible.

DOWNTIME

Dear Diary,

    During this time, I haven't been able to do my normal routine. Creating a stronger mental state of mind has been an essential task I have put at the top of my priorities. Also, continuing to stay physically fit is a key goal. With all of this time in my hands, I have challenged myself to continue to stay positive and learn something new about myself every day.

MAKING IT THROUGH ALONE

Dear Diary,

    Depression isn't really something I've ever prepared for or knew much about. So when it came, it came unexpectedly. I was juggling so much between school and organizations, a social life, and work.

    The first trigger of mine was money. I was working late hours at the library but only getting paid once a month. I take pride in being independent, so I hated asking my parents for help. I knew my mom had so much on her plate, so I tried alleviating some by keeping my needs to myself. I tried budgeting, but the only realistic solution was to make more money; but I had no time to.

    The second trigger was my social life. I was investing so much into "friends" that I saved no time for myself. I was receiving so much attention but no genuine love. What I needed was my true friends from back at home, but they had their own thing going on. I quickly learned that not all attention is good attention.

    And the third trigger was bottling everything up. I struggled with the idea of hurting other people's feelings, so I silenced all of my emotions to keep those around me happy.

    I took time alone on winter break to stop, think, and breathe. I worked another job and went in early in the mornings. I would break down in tears as soon as I clocked and didn't know why. I had no appetite and was forcing myself to eat. I had people around me that cared but that didn't know exactly what to say or how to help. I felt alone, although I wasn't. I felt like I was working through my situation off the strength of making sure I woke up to see another day. I would journal, video record, whatever I needed to do to see the next day. I rediscovered my hobbies, did things that made me happy at that moment. A few months later, I am happy, saying whatever it is I need to say, and making sure I don't fall back into that hole that I dug myself out of. The storm will pass, and the sun will shine again.

KEEP PUSHING!

Dear Diary,

One month ago, you couldn't have told me that the world would have been in pure panic due to a pandemic. As of March 2020, the only corona I knew about was the beer. Now, one month later, it seems every news channel, radio station, and living person is talking about corona, and not the good kind. As a millennial, I've heard stories about the recession and how it impacted the world; however, I never knew what it felt like to be in the start of one until COVID-19 started its course. It wasn't until I received the call from my employer stating they couldn't afford to keep me, and that day would be my last day. Did I realize, STUFF GOT REAL QUICKLY. Nowadays, my thoughts are more so on financial and mental stability. Trying to stay afloat while maintaining my grades seem harder and harder when I can barely find or afford necessities to get me through the week. Having long talks with God, family, and friends keep me going and help me remain positive. While I am not sure what the future may hold, I remain hopeful and positive that I will be able to walk across the stage in December and be able to breathe in fresh air without a mask.

PS: Never will I EVER take going outside for granted.

HEARTLESS WITH A BIG HEART

Dear Diary,

I am one of the most selfless people you will ever meet, someone that will give you the shirt off of their back, someone who will be a listening ear, or someone you can depend on no matter the situation.

In this world, we don't always receive the same energy that we give to others. You could say this is where my story originates from. I have experienced this through many friendships and even relationships. I know that this has caused me to become nonchalant and to hide my true feelings. And I hate that everyone can come to me when they are going through things, but I feel like I can't come to anyone. I struggle with opening up, but I don't want to be this heartless person with a big heart anymore.

THE FUNNY FRIEND

Dear Diary,

In my life, I feel like I always keep everyone laughing. I love to see others smile. I love seeing others happy. Am I happy?—tricky question. I would say, I experience the feeling of being lighter in certain situations, like when my best friend FaceTimes me to just tell me about his day, or when I'm out with my friends and it feels like the night may never end but in the best way.

But even in those situations, I find myself dissociating. I will literally blank out in the middle of a bar or at a sleepover with my friends because that feeling of lightness will disappear, and I'll begin to feel heavy again. So I block it out, humor—dark jokes, light jokes, buying my friends gifts for no reason—because how I was raised, if you want someone to know you love them or that you're sorry, you buy them things. I hate this idea. I hate materialism. But others seem to enjoy it, so I continue.

I'll make every joke and keep the room in the highest spirits despite my own because it makes me feel good to see others feel light. Does that make sense? I don't know. The thing about being the "funny friend" is we seem the happiest, right? We seem like we float on air and that we're always smiling and laughing. We're not. We want to be though.

We make really weird jokes sometimes. We can't handle extended periods of silence. Most people would say, we can be "overwhelming" and "too much sometimes." We don't mean to though. Dark thoughts consume us, and we just want to push them out, black them out, erase them. But unfortunately, dark thoughts are like deep stains. No amount of bleach can remove them or, in our case, no amount of anything. But laughter and smiles, they're like a beautiful, crazy rug that hides it. The rug is what we want you to see—bursts of color and spirits. But underneath? No, no, please don't lift it up. There's nothing you want underneath there. But eventually, those stains will seep through and get on the rug. So we bleach again. That's why some of our rugs are a little discolored.

For example, when we accidentally drink way more than our friends and start crying or when our friends express how "weird" they think we are, they say it lightheartedly, but we don't take it lightly. We close off and try to rewire again. Less talking, less attention, but keep the room light—new rug. Personally, I love being the funny friend. I love keeping people up because, for a moment, I too feel up. But sometimes, I also hate it. I hate the feeling of responsibility it causes me to be the person to blame for when things get annoying. I hate the feeling I get when people tell me I'm annoying or ask me why I laugh too hard for too long. It hurts. They think about it in the moment; I think about it for at least a month. I'm getting offtrack so basically.

Social distancing has made it extremely hard to be the funny friend. I don't have a group around me to tell jokes to in order to block out the dark and consuming thoughts. I'm scared when this is over, I may be too overwhelming because of how much isolation this has caused me. I miss being the funny friend. I miss making my friends laugh. I miss not feeling like this. I don't know what my rug will look like when this is over, and I'm scared.

NERVOUS

Dear Diary,

    The future is usually something to look forward to. But as of now, I am nervous. It seems like I had life all figured out. And then a pandemic came and put my life on pause. It honestly has put my anxiety through the roof. "Graduation" is a month away, and I have no clue of what I plan to do with my degree and the rest of my life. Prayer and my family are the only things keeping me sane these days. To anyone else going through the same thing, it's okay to not have everything figured out.
    Take a deep breath, and God will direct you down the right path.

STRESSED

Dear Diary,

    Lately, I've been stressed out. Sometimes I find myself unable to think clearly because I have had so much on my plate. Having all my classes online doesn't make it any better. I haven't been outside unless I'm going straight to work. Other than that, I am stuck in the house doing work. I literally start my day at 9:40 a.m., and I have class and schoolwork until 5:40 p.m. Then I have work from 6:00 p.m. until 12:00 a.m. By the time I get home, I don't feel like doing anything, so I go straight to sleep. I try to stay on top of my schoolwork, which I am doing an okay job. I've missed two assignments already, and I am not proud of it. I wish I could have a break. I feel like I stare at a computer screen all day doing assignments for school. Work isn't fun either since I changed my schedule to night shift. It sucks doing everything virtually. I miss my social life—hanging out with friends, going to class on campus, and going out and not having to wear a mask. I guess I am just trying to cope with everything. Hopefully, things will get better because I barely have the motivation to stay on top of things.

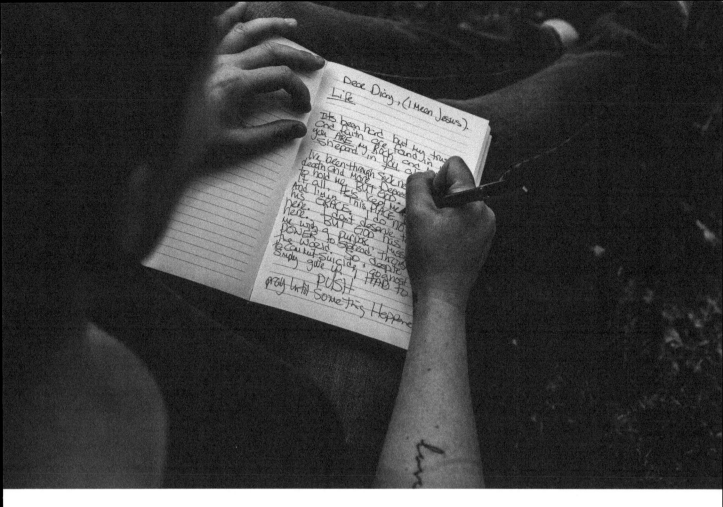

BUT GOD

Dear Diary (I mean Jesus),

    Life—it's been hard, but my trust and faith are found in you. You ARE my ROCK and my Shepherd. In You alone, I trust. I've been through sickness, pain, abuse, death, and more. Depression TRIED to hold me BUT GOD. Through it all, He's kept me, protected me. And I'm in THIS PLACE because of His GRACE. I do not belong here. I don't deserve to be here. BUT GOD has inflicted me with a purpose, mission, and POWER to spread throughout the world. So despite wanting to commit suicide, "go ghost," or simply give up, I HAD TO PUSH (pray until something happened)—push through the pain. And NOW I can say that I AM BLESSED. I lack nor beg for anything because GOD is MY Provider.

TIME

Dear Diary,

    During this time, I've watched myself create every excuse to not be alone, like going out of my way to be surrounded by some type of noise that'll keep me distracted long enough to watch the day expire then waking up to do it all over again the next day. I've noticed that being busy was a way to blindfold reality, enough to not focus on the things that I didn't want to find time to fix, that slowing down long enough would force me to take responsibility for the wounds that I've allowed to stay open for too long. I've spent too much time admiring sunflowers in other gardens that I've forgotten the importance of tending to my own.

TOXIC

Dear Diary,

    I was in a toxic relationship for about two years. Now I have been in a somewhat great relationship for about two years. I keep searching for things that are wrong with the person I am currently with, and I don't know why. Most of the times, I accept that this person is just really great. But every time my significant other does something wrong, I blow it way out of proportion. In my past relationship, something horrible was always happening to me, but I felt like I really loved this person. They treated me horribly and still treat me bad even though we are no longer together. I still want my ex in my life, and I don't know why. I wish I could cut all ties; but for some reason, I can't. Even after he/she does malicious things to me, I still accept him/her as a friend. My family even hated my ex, and they love my current significant other. I do feel like I have truly moved on, and I don't want to be in a relationship with my ex at all. But I wonder why I keep thinking about her/him. I feel like I sort of liked the toxicity of the relationship.

THE STRAIN OF SOCIAL DISTANCING

Dear Diary,

As we go longer and longer in the stay-at-home order, I have seen the stain it has caused. We are a culture of social creatures that are not meant to be in solitaire. We are meant to interact with others. That's why, as far back as history can go, we have lived in communities and groups all across the lands. We are meant to lean on others to help us get through our day and need the love of family to keep us safe and going. I have seen husbands and wives filing for divorce because they cannot stand being in the same house now, or their lovers have come out of hiding because they cannot go seeking around under lockdown. I have seen myself struggle to keep our kids entertained at home plus trying to get them to understand they have to keep studying even though they are not in a classroom. I have really been struggling and stressing to keep my grades up with school. I have cried many nights because I think I'm going to fail one of my classes due to not being on campus. I am a hands-on learner, not online. And trying to do your work with a classmate because it's a partner project is very difficult. Plus trying to keep up with my son's schoolwork, keeping my house in order and still going to work have made me feel more overwhelmed than ever. I try to see this from both sides and understand people really want to get back to normal, but we also have to keep those at risk safe too. I understand that some people think their freedom is being taken away, but this is not forever. I feel bad for those in leadership positions because they are having to make very difficult decisions for the whole country. All in all, I, myself, am ready to get back to some normalcy due to my mental state. I want the stress and crying to stop. If anything, I would love a reset button for 2020.

THE GOOD LISTENER

Dear Diary,

It can be hard being a good listener sometimes. The more you listen, the more people come to you with their problems. We need to normalize asking "Are you in a good headspace for me to talk about my problems to you?" Here's some advice for anyone reading: check on the people that check on you the most. Sometimes we're not okay. Sometimes we can be going through more than we can bear. Sometimes we want to talk too instead of JUST listen.

> Get up and face the day even if you're only facing it half awake.
>
> —US university student

GROWING APART

Dear Diary,

    I've spent so much time investing myself into a relationship that was going nowhere. I wasn't happy, and it seemed like I only wanted to make things work because of the history we previously shared together. High school sweethearts—we had our future all planned out. We discussed going to college, being established in our careers, getting married, and even having children one day. Sounds amazing right? Well, things don't always go as we plan in life.

    College added distance between us and made us grow apart. Argument after argument, it began adding additional stress on top of juggling classwork and multiple organizations on campus. I was being drained mentally and emotionally every time we talked. Recently, I decided that enough was enough and decided to end my on-and-off relationship with my ex.

    My ex continues to try and come back in my life from time to time, but I am happy to move forward without looking back. Since then, I have been seeing nothing but growth in my life. Initially, I thought this decision would break me, but it ended up being the decision I needed to help me build myself back up. I have learned that doing what's best for you isn't selfish, it's self-care.

A WAKE-UP CALL

Dear Diary,

Yesterday was a very peaceful day, at least I thought it was going to be. I had my phone on "Do Not Disturb" for a good chunk of my day, and it appeared as though nothing could disturb me or bother me in any way. After finishing up a few assignments that I had due this week, I decided to take my phone off "Do Not Disturb" and to go for a peaceful car ride around my city. Little did I know, this was where my peace would quickly end.

Maybe fifteen minutes into my "peaceful" car ride and a quick stop by Chick-fil-A, I received a phone call from my manager. I immediately knew that it couldn't be good because my manager NEVER calls me. I was right; it wasn't good news at all. She informed me that "all part-time employees would be losing their jobs because the company will be unable to continue to pay us while we're away."

If someone could physically see my heart at that moment, they would have seen it shatter as soon as I heard the news. I was devastated. I've had this job for nearly three years. I have never been laid off from a job in my entire life, so it was a new and frustrating feeling. It's an even scarier feeling knowing that my lease will be up at the end of July, and I will be graduating in the next few weeks.

I cried tears of hurt, frustration, and overall fear of what was next to come. After crying, I prayed. I already thought about getting a better job after I graduated, and I planned to start looking in my field. I believe that everything happens for a reason and that I could have been keeping my previous job to stay in my comfort zone. I'm trying to become more positive about the situation and use this as motivation to look for a better job—a job with better benefits that pays more and maybe even a job in my field. The call from my manager was so unexpected, but it could have been the wake-up call I needed to answer.

ONLY TIME WILL TELL

Dear Diary,

    I decided to quarantine with my family because I usually don't get to see them as much during the school year. A typical day is busy, and it involves me having classes, work, or even meetings sometimes. Because of this, I'm not usually around my family for more than the holidays or special occasions. I thought it would be a good idea for me to make up for lost times. I have an older brother that has been diagnosed with bipolar disorder, so I never know what to expect once I visit my family. It's almost like flipping a coin. We've always had a close relationship, but everything changed once I came to college. He always wants to pick an argument or blames me for how his life is going. My brother and I are the complete opposite. I can honestly say that I'm a little more obedient to our parents, made better grades, and I am a little more mature even though I'm the youngest. While I've been at home, there have been really good days, and there have been really bad days.

    This particular bad day really hurt me. He picked an argument with me and said some hurtful things. In his eyes, "I'm our parent's favorite," "they treat him like he's stupid every time I come into town," and "I think I am better than him." All of this was said, followed by a series of curse words that I'll leave out of this story. It's hard hearing all of these hurtful words from someone that's supposed to love you the most. I'll graduate in a few weeks, and it hurts knowing that my own older brother isn't supportive of me. I feel like he will just look at this as another way of me "feeling like I'm better than him." I couldn't take it anymore, and I chose to leave our parent's house the next day. I hate that I had to leave so soon, but I couldn't take it anymore. I'm praying that things get better with time and that one day we can be as close as we were before I came to college.

FINDING MY PEACE

Dear Diary,

    My sophomore year, I was always agitated and short-tempered. I argued a lot and was known as a "hothead." I learned that I couldn't continue life being that way. It took me almost losing one of my longest friendships to get me to realize that my actions were getting out of hand. I found a new church home, began meditating, and also found a new hobby that relaxes me. It's hard for me to get mad nowadays; and when I do get mad, I know how to handle it in a better way. Finding my peace has probably been the best thing I could have ever discovered.

I WILL

Dear Diary,

    I WILL find my purpose in this world. I WILL be happy eventually. I WILL find the person that is meant to be with me. I WILL be financially stable. I WILL get through ALL my hard times. They don't last forever. I WILL love myself more. I WILL put myself before others, and I WILL be selfish if I have to. I WILL NOT let anyone run over me. I AM BEAUTIFUL, and anybody who can't see that is missing out on a blessing. I WILL regain my strength mentally, physically, and emotionally. I WILL find trust, and I WILL be able to trust others fully. I WILL lose weight, and I WILL find my healthy weight. I WILL build a stronger relationship and bond with God. I AM God's child. I WILL succeed.

THIS IS MY STORY

Dear Diary,

    This is my story; I hope it helps someone else however they need it to. Thank you for having a safe space for me to share.

    I was raped inside a dorm on a college campus I attended before I came here. He was my classmate. And when we were alone, he took his opportunity and changed my life forever.

    Afterward, I was scared and traumatized and reported what happened to the college and the police, but no one believed me. The female officer responsible for taking my statement interrogated me like I was the criminal and then deemed it wasn't even a crime. She called it an unwanted one-night stand. In the end, she decided nothing criminal transpired, and my case was closed without the offender ever being questioned.

    My world instantly fell apart. I suffered through flashbacks, panic attacks, nightmares that led me to start cutting myself in the same places he left bruises as a means to control my suffering and pain. I couldn't eat; and every night, I cried myself to sleep, listening to all the voices taking over my mind. "I don't believe you," "you deserved it," "it's your fault," "you should have kept quiet." They had it all wrong, and I couldn't believe they treated me like I was nothing.

    Things got so bad. I started to think about ending my life. And truth be told, I tried. Realizing I needed help, I started to see a therapist and was diagnosed with PTSD, anxiety, and depression. I still had to see him every day on campus. He was everywhere—in my classes, hanging out with my friends, making an effort to torture me on a daily basis. And there was nothing—absolutely nothing—I could do about it. And there was nothing anyone did about it.

    I remember being so tired, having to pretend I was fine when all I wanted to do was scream out loud to be heard. No one believed me, and I still had to see him every day, and I hated my life. He impacted everything I did, and I was deteriorating.

    Slowly over the next few years, with the help of the therapist, I started to take back control of my life. I changed colleges, and I realized I was worth fighting for and that I would fight for all the other women who have been forced to go through being shamed for speaking up.

    I am only one person, but I want to make as much noise about what happened to me and use my voice so loudly. I can create change because it is my hope that no one will ever have to go through what I endured.

CHECKING IN

Dear Diary,

    Checking in with the people you love is so important to me. At least once a week, I try to send out thoughtful texts, check in to see how people are doing, or I even make sure they know that I love them. I had a friend that passed away this past year, and he would always be the friend to check in on everyone. He was such an amazing friend—so thoughtful, caring, and loving. And I truly wish I would have appreciated it more back then. He had pushed me to become a better person to people every chance that I get. He taught me that checking in can go a long way. A simple text or call can make a big difference. I still have all of our old text messages, and I revisit them sometimes. 'Til this day, I wish I could get one more text message from him checking in on me.

I BEAT CANCER TODAY—WHAT DID YOU DO?

Dear Diary,

With all the insanity going on, being separated from so many of my family, and now graduation postponed, I should be sad.

But I'm not.

Today, I got the call. I beat cancer. Yes, I said it. I beat cancer. It's so hard not to share with my friends. But the truth is, I never did share; so hopefully, through this entry, everyone who will read will celebrate. For two years, it was unknown to anyone—my friends, my professors, my classmates. But I have been fighting something so much bigger than what I felt people would understand, so I fought silently.

Two years ago, summer was spent having two surgeries and then radiation. I didn't think I could come back for my junior year, but I did. It was hard. I was scared—too scared. I thought no one would understand, so I didn't share. I didn't share I could no longer have babies. I didn't share I couldn't walk across campus without being in pain from the surgery. I didn't share why I didn't want to go out and eat. All I wanted to do was find that end goal of graduation and getting the all clear. When I rang the bell after my last treatment, I rang it alone. But I was still so proud. The waiting game to get the final "all clear" came today—just in time for graduation. It's MY graduation gift to myself. It's MY triumph. And while I would tell anyone who asked me to always find your support group, today was MY day. I am celebrating, and I am sharing my celebration with you.

To whoever may read this, never give up on your dreams. Love harder. Dance sillier. Pray with great fervor. Giggle every day. Just never EVER give up.

I BEAT CANCER today. What did you do?

Now for that master's degree…

Nutrition Facts

Serving Size   larger than life
Servings Per Container 1

Amount Per Serving	
Calories Unlimited	**Calories from Love**

	% Daily Value
Total Satisfaction	100%
Passion	100%
Happiness	100%
Creativity	100%
Wonder	100%
Self-Esteem	100%
Integrity	100%
Empathy	100%
Patience	100%
Relationships	100%
Rest	100%
Fitness	100%
Taking Action	100%

* Percent daily values are based on fully accepting the now and living in the present. Actual daily values may be higher or lower depending on lifestyle, focus, personal development, stress levels, and overall sense of purpose.

HAPPY WEIGHT

Dear Diary,

    Growing up, I never had to worry about my weight. I was an athlete; so naturally, I was fit. I could eat anything I wanted to in the world without having to fear that I would gain any weight. I can definitely say that changed once I came to college. I wanted to strictly focus on school, so I didn't even attempt to play basketball at a collegiate level. As I adjusted to not being as active as I was in high school, my body adjusted as well. I gained weight slowly but surely as the weeks flew by. I wasn't the fit girl that everyone once knew me as back home. It was a hard adjustment, and it has even made me extremely self-conscious at one point in my life. I didn't want to eat. I thought that maybe if I ate less, I would stop gaining weight, and my body would go back to how it used to be. I was making myself sick. I was always light-headed and felt physically weak because I stopped eating as much. After nearly passing out around a group of close friends, I had to finally confess what I had been going through. I talked to them and told them that I didn't like the way my body looked. They really helped me feel better about myself and helped me realize that I was being too hard on myself. My weight didn't change who I was as a person, and it didn't change how anyone else treated me. I looked at myself a completely different way after that conversation I had with my close friends. I love the woman I see in the mirror now, and I finally don't stress about a little weight gain every now and then.

CHANGE IS INEVITABLE

Dear Diary,

    "You've changed"—a statement I've heard recently that I can't get over. Change shouldn't always be viewed as a negative aspect. Change can be beautiful. I love the change that can't be seen with the visual eye. Some people think that being a strong person means that someone is physically strong. Strength comes in many forms, and I had to become stronger mentally. Verbal abuse can be just as damaging as physical abuse, and I'm grateful for change because I found the strength to never go back to someone who has broken me. I recently left a toxic relationship, and I am not that same fragile girl anymore. I changed for the better.

CROSSING THE FINISH LINE

Dear Diary,

Today I submitted my last assignment on D2L. I've waited for this moment for a long time, five years long to be exact. I'm a few days away from achieving an accomplishment that I thought would never get here. The thought of all those long nights spent in the James E. Walker Library is finally about to pay off. My path to get to this point right now was not an easy journey. I changed my major twice, failed a class, lost my Hope scholarship, and nearly lost hope for finishing school. I was honestly frustrated and stressed, but this was the eustress I needed to make me turn my situation around. I discovered a major that I love, and I changed my study habits. After I regained my Hope scholarship, I have been on the dean's list every semester. It's not always where you start but where you finish.

To anyone reading this, I will be a graduate the next time you see me. Never give up! Crawl until you can walk, and walk until you can run to the finish line, but never quit.

NEW BEGINNINGS

Dear Diary,

    I'm in search for something new. There are times when I just want to fill my car up and drive to a completely different state to start over—a new city, new environment, new people, somewhere no one knows me, and that my problems and pain can't follow me. My life may have begun in Tennessee, but I know that it isn't meant to end here. I have big dreams, and being in Tennessee makes me feel like I'll never get the chance to achieve them. I feel stuck being here, almost like I have no more room for growth here.

    As graduation approaches, I am searching for a new beginning.

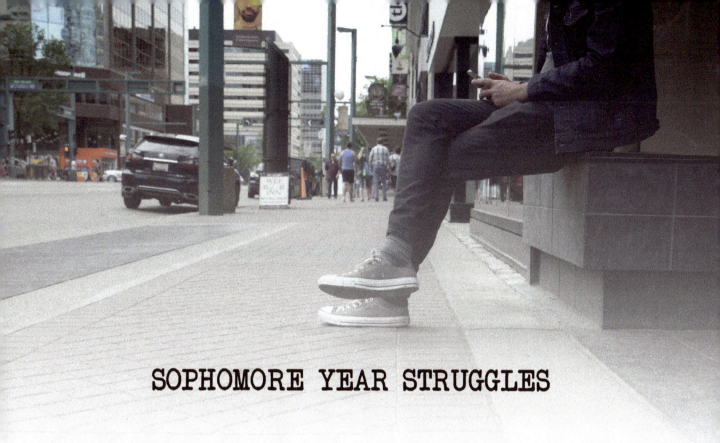

SOPHOMORE YEAR STRUGGLES

Dear Diary,

After getting acclimated to MTSU's campus, I decided to become more involved on campus my sophomore year. During this year, my sibling got into trouble financially, and my parents stepped in to help. They would always complain of how much money they spent, and it made me feel uncomfortable to ask for any money at all. I didn't want to add on to their stress. Becoming more involved on campus left me with less time to work than usual, and I didn't want my grades to slip either. Things got overwhelming to the point I had to choose focusing on school than working. I was used to bringing in extra money so that I wouldn't have to ask my parents for anything while I was at school. It got hard; I was living on campus, so I never had to worry about paying for gas. But food was a different story. I was barely eating, and I was starting to lose a lot of weight. I would go all day without eating so that I could limit myself to one meal a day. It was cheaper, but it also forced me to go throughout the day starving. I got to the point that I was signing up for food birthday freebies. A lot of my friends were wondering why I would always eat the same meals over and over. It wasn't because it was my favorite food, it was because it was free food. My parents grew concerned once they saw how small I was getting. I eventually broke down crying and telling them that I wasn't eating a lot and the reason that I never came to them about it. It was hard to talk about that to my parents, but I'm glad I finally did. They are more understanding and even apologized for making me feel like I couldn't come to them for anything. It's a time in my life that I try to erase from my memory, but I'm glad that I don't have that struggle anymore.

UNTITLED JOURNEY

Dear Diary,

    Life is unpredictable and can take you anywhere. I never thought, in a million years, that I would be at MTSU, and I never thought I would be nine days away from graduating. A lot of my friends back home has dropped out of college, and some of them have even been arrested. A lot of my friends from where they are let them affect where they are going in life. That wasn't the life I wanted to live. I chose to stick it out no matter how hard things were. I knew I couldn't let my parents down, and I couldn't let myself down. So far, I have been on the right track, and I have been making good choices. I don't know where life will take me next, but I know I'll continue to move forward and never backward.

DON'T BE AFRAID TO TRY AGAIN

Dear Diary,

    I have always enjoyed being engaged in hands-on learning experiences other than in class settings. During my sophomore year, I applied to a prestigious internship. I really wanted to get this internship, and it would work out perfectly since it is in the summer. I was going to be able to work in a billion-dollar business. Sadly, I never heard from the organization. Toward the end of school that year, I realized that I did not get that internship. I definitely was crushed, but I did not allow that to get my spirits down. The next year, I knew I was going to try again. However, this time, I was going to come out a lot stronger. I remade my resume, cover letter, and got some more references. I already had the experience from working my side job I worked in college. So this time, it was three years of that experience instead of two. Once I applied for the second, it took a while before I heard something back from the organization. Although it took some time, I finally heard back from them. They informed me that I got an interview that I needed to get it scheduled. I got it done as quickly as possible and nailed the interview. I was notified that I got the internship and that I would start in the summer!

WHAT A YEAR!

Dear Diary,

    Since spring break first started, things were going just fine. Classes were in full swing, grades were looking great, social activities on campus were lively, and MT was the place to be. Though the coronavirus was not weighed upon as seriously at the time, the time for discomfort would come at some point. We went on spring break as scheduled and didn't think nothing beyond that. Eventually, the week was over, and we were informed there would be another added week, giving us an additional streak break. Here we were thinking, *This would be great*; but in reality, it was the complete opposite. Upon the second week being over, we were informed from President McPhee that campus would resume remotely and online for the remainder of the semester. That was when I knew things were going bad. Who knew what was next? We for sure didn't. I don't think anyone did either and with all this coming to life. That was when 2020 as a whole took a turn. The US went into a national quarantine phase in which basically the entire country was out into a lockdown, not only from ourselves but from the rest of the world. Seniors didn't graduate the way they wanted, spring events were canceled, and so much more. It was a complete mess. We knew from that point, the rest of the year would be different as well. Fast forward to fall 2020, and we are all virtual, hybrid, online, socially distanced students just trying to pass classes. There's no telling how the spring will look, better yet this winter. All we can do is hope and pray for better days.

A YEAR IN REVIEW

Dear Diary,

    Never did I expect my freshman year to look like this. Of course, never did I expect my senior year to look as it did either. It's almost fascinating at times to think about how the compilations of the "year in review" will look on December 31, 2020. For me, it was a strange spring, which turned into a desperate summer; and now I am at a new school with few friends under sometimes the strangest of circumstance. It sounds a little depressing, but it's really not. Somehow through all this, I grew up a little. I was able to appreciate the most important things more and reassess the lesser important things that seemed to always fog my mind and my judgments. I am only eighteen years old, but I feel like an old soul whom society forced me to grow up sooner than I planned to. I was all about the freshman year parties and being the social seeker. Strange or not, these last six months make me want to slow down and think harder about my future, how to make society better for the next freshman class, and make kindness a motto. College is about lasting memories, but it's the focus of those lasting memories that I want to reassess. Life has certainly challenged me with my thoughts in this chaos of society, so I receive the challenge and will strive to make whoever walks in my shadow a better place. So here's to my personal "year in review" and where I am on December 31, 2020. Bring on #TrueBlue.

THE FINALE

Dear Diary,

So there was this guy. I know what you're thinking. It's not a sob story, so just stick around. Me and this guy had a great connection and a strong bond. We established a solid friendship, and things were fine until he notified me that he had feelings for me and that he would love to "be with me." So I let him know that I had feelings for him too and that we could begin to further our friendship. The problem is, every time I looked up, he was with another woman. As you can tell, that caused great confusion on my end, being that he has expressed his interest in me. However, I decided to tough it out and still be the great friend I have been and think maybe it'll eventually happen.

Time passed several months. At this point, the idea of a relationship with this friend was out the window, plus he was dating someone. So I vowed to keep the friendship platonic and move on. However, every chance he got, he told me how he felt about me and that he'd "love to be with me." After a repetitive cycle of him confessing his feelings but never committing, I ended the friendship. I could've kept the friendship had he not continuously cross the platonic boundaries without a commitment. It was either be my platonic friend with no mind games or be with me. I realized that my feelings are not meant to be toyed with. I realized that I am worth more than someone who can't make their mind up.

To my ladies, please do not let people toy with you. If a man wants you, he will show you. Don't wait for him to change his mind or realize that you are that woman. People tend to take kindness for weakness. They take advantage of the fact that you'll always be there, so they do as they please—not anymore. Command your respect, for you have given yours. Speak up against the tarnishing of your heart. Even if you two have history, if it hinders you from becoming the best you that you can be, let it go.

Signed: a happy black woman

ACKNOWLEDGMENTS

Special thanks to Middle Tennessee State University for piloting Untold: The Campus Diaries project.

Very special thanks to Cynthia Chafin of MTSU's Center for Health and Human Services and to Monica, Jaida, and Samantha for their dedication to the vision, creation, and development of Untold: The Campus Diaries.

The people represented in the photos do not reflect the individual stories. All photos were taken by Lorna Dancey and Karen Shayne.

For more information on Untold: The Campus Diaries and the *Campus Diaries Exhibit*, contact us at UNTOLDProject.org.

ABOUT THE AUTHORS

The UNTOLD team of Karen Shayne and Lorna Dancey began in 2019 through the introduction of a mutual friend who witnessed two powerful visionaries from different countries sharing the same passion for storytelling.

Karen Shayne of Nashville, Tennessee, is a media publisher and producer. With countless awards and features in numerous magazines, Karen's passion for finding human-interest stories has led her around the world to find and share stories that inspire and motivate.

Lorna Dancey is a photographer, writer, and storyteller from Alberta, Canada. Her work is poignant, and the compelling projects she creates are visionary and compassion-based. The plight of others and the determination to help each and every person through her lens and storytelling lays the foundation for her work.

Through their collaborative efforts of UNTOLD, both women have dedicated their lives to tirelessly advocating for the silent voice to be heard. Together, their mission is to build a bridge, not just between two countries through story sharing but to invite a sense of unity among all nations to inspire hope and healing. UNTOLD isn't only about giving hope but also helping others see beyond their limitations and creating a domino effect for positive change, harmony, and mutual compassion. Learn more about the UNTOLD Project at UNTOLDProject.org.

CPSIA information can be obtained
at www.ICGtesting.com
Printed in the USA
LVHW071938290422
717571LV00023B/1638